THE DREAMER IN YOU

8 INSPIRATIONAL STORIES ON FAITH, PURPOSE AND LIVING THE DREAM!

COMPILED BY
KISHMA A. GEORGE

The Dreamer in You

8 Inspirational Stories on Faith, Purpose and Living the Dream

© September 2023

By K.A.G. (Kishma A. George Enterprises)

Published in the United States of America

by

www.cb-publishing.com

Cover design D'Vine Designs

Scripture quotations marked (AMP) are taken from the Amplified Bible, Copyright © 2015 by The Lockman Foundation. Used by permission.

Scripture quotations marked (NLT) are taken from the Holy Bible, New Living Translation, copyright © 1996, 2004, 2007, 2013, 2015 by Tyndale House Foundation. Used by permission of Tyndale House Publishers, Inc., Carol Stream, Illinois 60188. All rights reserved.

Scripture quotations marked (NCV) are taken from the New Century Version. Copyright © 2005 by Thomas Nelson, Inc. Used by permission. All rights reserved.

Scripture quotations marked (NIV) are taken from the Holy Bible, New International Version®, NIV®. Copyright © 1973, 1978, 1984, 2011 by Biblica, Inc.™ Used by permission of Zondervan. All rights reserved worldwide. www.zondervan.com

Scripture quotations marked NLV are taken from the New Life Version, Copyright © 1969 and 2003. Used by permission of Barbour Publishing, Inc., Uhrichsville, Ohio 44683. All rights reserved.

Scripture quotations marked MSG are taken from The Message, copyright © 1993, 2002, 2018 by Eugene H. Peterson. Used by permission of NavPress. All rights reserved. Represented by Tyndale House Publishers

Scripture quotations marked (TLB) are taken from The Living Bible, copyright © 1971 by Tyndale House Foundation. Used by permission of Tyndale House Publishers, Carol Stream, Illinois 60188. All rights reserved.

All rights reserved under International Copyright Law. Contents and/or cover may not be reproduced, distributed, or transmitted in any form or by any means or stored in a database or retrieval system, without the prior written consent of the publisher and/or authors.

ISBN: 978-1-945377-31-0

First Edition Printing

Printed in the United States of America

September 2023

Table of Contents

Birth the Dreamer in You By Kishma A. George — 1

Harness Your Passion By Jacqueline C. Griffith — 13

Dreaming in the Dark By Dr. Shavona Whitehead — 23

I Dare to Dream By Simra Dalmida — 39

The Dreamer In You By Tiffany McCullough — 51

I Am The Dream Walking By Dr. Nephetina L. Serrano — 65

It Will Happen For You By Shamika Minisee — 83

Seven Keys to Dream Management & Stewardship
By Dr. Nicckay Natson — 93

Birth the Dreamer in You

By Kishma A. George

Several months after I disconnected myself from the dream killers and began working on the vision, I remember sitting in the chair in my living room and the Lord gave me an assignment to host a fundraiser event for the non-profit organization. I was very excited about the project. I informed the Board Members and other people about the project. We started to plan four months ahead of the event. Everything was going well; the vendors registered and we got the funds for the location of the event, and the fliers to advertise the event were ready to be distributed. Everything you can think of was done to have a successful event.

The day of the event came and I was very excited because, in my mind, the team had done a GREAT job marketing the event and I thought HUNDREDS of people would show up. The event started at 9:00 a. m. and by the time it turned 2:00 pm., only 30 people showed up in a facility that can hold over 500 people. After the event, I went home so disappointed with tears in my eyes. I felt as if I never wanted to come out of my bed again and face the Board Members or the world. The event, in my eyes, was truly a flop and not successful. I felt like a BIG failure. I told myself I would never host another event again for the rest of my life.

One day during prayer, I was crying out to God, asking why the event was not successful and what I did wrong. The Lord laid in my heart the thought that the event was a success because I completed the project. He reminded me that numbers did not matter but how the event was organized with excellence that mattered. The Lord also reminded me to DREAM Again! Just because it did not work out the way I think it should go does not mean it was unsuccessful. God was teaching me to become successful, you have to learn from your failures, what to do, and what not to do. Moreover, the more you do anything, the better you become as you go along. God was teaching me that He is guiding, leading, and encouraging me not to give up and Dream Big!

The following year, the Lord laid in my heart to host another fundraiser event. I began this time first by seeking the face of God for instructions and directions. I made many changes to the things I did at the last event. I worked harder and marketed the event differently than I did at the first event. At this second event, we had over 200 people; there were more vendors and more tickets were sold. The event was TRULY a BIG success! So, I want to encourage you today that when you have a dream, do not give up even if you lose money pursuing your dreams, people walking out on you, no one wanting to fund your dreams, lack of support, etc. DREAM Again & DREAM BIG!!

Some of you reading this book, God showed you a vision that you would open a business, publish a book, write songs, teach, preach, open a shelter, write stage plays, open a non-profit, make-up line, clothing store, shoe store, a mini mall, mentor, produce music, write poetry, etc., and you ask God, "Can it really happened?" God is saying, "Yes…if you only Believe! God wants to bring forth the Dreamer in YOU! Remember, with God all things are POSSIBLE! God wants us to Dream outside the box; Eph. 3:20 states, "Now unto us who is able to do exceeding abundantly above all that we ask or think; according to the power that worketh in us." God's Word plainly and clearly stated our purpose, which is to be God's hands on this earth.

God wants you to succeed, and if you are willing to step up to the plate, you will not fail, because God will never leave you nor forsake you.

To every dreamer reading this, I want to encourage you to DREAM AGAIN!! When you have a dream, walk by faith and not by sight. The belief that dreams are impossible to achieve stops people from getting what they really want. People are what they believe themselves to be. Proverbs 23:7 says, "For as he thinketh in his heart, so is he!" If you want success, start thinking of yourself as a success. True success is the progressive achievement of your God-inspired goals. Success is the result of living in alignment with God's laws of success. God did not make you with limitations. Mark 9:23 says, "All things are possible to him that believeth." Believe that new and exciting opportunities are coming your way in this NEW SEASON because God is not through with blessing you! Whatever vision God has showed you, believe His Word and step out in faith until it is manifested in your life.

There were seasons in my life when while pursuing my dreams, I asked God to guide me through my trials and tribulations. I remember one day, I was facing a situation that looked impossible! I had no money to buy food or items that I needed for the home.

Even though I was working a full-time job, my money did not cover all of my expenses & food. I could not apply for Food Stamps because, based on the system, I was making too much money but was stuck. I cried out to the Lord to help m. I thought I should call the guy I dated several years ago and he will send the money. But deep down inside, I could not do it. That week I remember my daughter turning to me and saying, Mommy, God will help us. During that week, I checked the mailbox as I normally don't check the mailbox every day because of all the bills, so I usually wait weeks before I check the mailbox. But that week I checked the mailbox, there was a check in the mail from a Company stating that over the years they had overcharged me, and they owed me money! When I opened the checked, I cried & cried with Joy, knowing that God would supply my needs.

Dreamers we have to know that everything depends on believing God. We cannot do anything without a living faith. If we only knew the power of God then we won't doubt that he would always come through for us! The Word of God is life. God moves as you believe. Remember, Faith is a "substance" of things hope for, it is an evidence of things not seen" (Hebrews 11:1). It brings about what you cannot see and brings forth what is not there. God took the Word and made the world in 6 days. Jesus, the Word of God, made that which has not been made by the Word. God wants to bring us into that blessed place of faith, changing us into a real substance of faith until we believe in our hearts that whatever we ask, believing, we will receive. I love reading (Acts 6:8) because Stephen was truly a man of faith. God manifested Himself in Stephen's body that he was full of faith and power and did great wonders and signs among the people. God could do mighty things through him because he dares to believe God. God could fulfill His purpose through Stephen's life because he believed all things are possible with God.

As Dreamers, God wants to do great things through your life in this season for His kingdom. There are assignments God has specifically called you to do that no one else in the world can do. God wants you to believe that all things are possible with Him. So, no matter where you are in life and you feel stuck, believe God has a way of making every crooked way straight and your steps are ordered by God. God hands are upon you to birth your dreams. You might feel like Daniel in the lion's den or Shadrach, Meshach and Abednego thrown in the fire. Remember, you will birth out greatness through the fire and the storm. You will begin to see God move in your life like never. The things you had to endure were to increase your faith in God.

There are days when we as dreamers need to have our faith strengthened, and it becomes imperative for us to recognize that God has designed the just to live by faith. We have to remember that God's Word is sufficient. One word from God can change a nation. God's Word is "from everlasting to everlasting." I believe God wants to bring you to a definite place of unwavering faith and confidence in Himself as you pursue your God-given Dreams. I remember working on a project, and the non- profit had to come up with $2000.00. I began to pray and continue to stand on the Word of God. Weeks went by and there was no sign that the organization could come up with the $2000.00. One day as I was driving home, the Holy Spirit told me to check the non-profit organization mailbox. Mind you, it was after 10:00pm at night, but I listened and went to the mailbox.

I want to encourage you, dreamers, that when the Holy Spirit speaks to your heart, just obey. We often miss God's blessing because we don't move when God speaks to us and our dreams are delayed. We have to move when God speaks first time to us, and things will flow much better and easier in our lives. When I got to the mailbox and opened it, it was a letter package from a company. As I opened the first envelope in the package, there was a paper that said, "here is ways you can receive funds by using our fundraising package." I began to put the package down and the Holy Spirit spoke to me and said continue looking inside the envelope. As I looked inside the envelope, there was another envelope with another white envelope and when I finally got to the last envelope, inside it was a $2000.00 check. I began to scream and cry and said God THANK YOU!!! You are truly faithful to your Word! So, I encourage every dreamer today that no matter what your bank account looks like right now, remember God will always give you provision for your vision. Believe, Believe, Believe! God wants to move supernaturally in your life right now and show you that He is truly Dreaming through your eyes! With God, all things are possible! Dream Big and BIRTH out the Dreamer in You!

Dr. Kishma's Acknowledgements:

First and foremost, I want to give God all the glory and honor, as He made this vision possible. I love You, Lord, with all my heart! 🩶In memory of my beloved father, Edmond Felix George; I am thankful for his encouragement and inspiring me to dream.🩶

To the best mother in the world, Novita Scatliffe-George; I thank you for your love, support, encouraging words and praying for me. Thank you for not giving up on me. I love you, Mom! 🩶

To My wonderful daughter Kiniquá, I love you dearly. Thank you for your encouraging words, hugs and love. 🩶

To my family—James, Raeisha, Christopher, Joshua, Seriah, Janisha and Kayla —thank you for supporting the vision with your prayers and love. 🩶

Thank you Toy James and Abena McClean for your prayers, support and encouraging me to pursue my dreams. I thank God that you are my special friends. Love you, ladies. 🩶

A special thank you to the co-authors of The Dreamer in You; Dr. Shavona Whitehead, Simra Dalmida, Dr.Nicckay Natson, Tiffany McCullough, Shamika Minisee, Jacqueline Griffith, Dr. Nephetina Serrano 🩶

A special thank you to my beautiful Jackie Hicks for her amazing photography and beautiful Letitia Thornhill for her gift of makeup artist! Love you, ladies! 🩶

To K.I.S.H. Home, Inc.'s board/advisors, volunteers and mentors; thank you for your dedication, support and believing in the vision of helping make a difference in the lives of young women in Delaware. ♥

To Emily Ann Warren, thank you for your support, love, and believing in me.

To Prophetess Ayanna, publisher; I thank God every day for bringing you into my life. You have been a blessing. Thank you for your encouraging words, support, love and believing in the vision. Love you. ♥

Lastly, but not least, I would like to thank D'Vine Designs, ChosenButterfly Publishing and everyone who has encouraged, prayed for and supported K.I.S.H. Home, Inc. over the years, I am forever grateful. God Bless! ♥♥♥

Dr. Kishma A. George

Dr. Kishma A. George can, in a single phrase, be described as a Purpose Pusher. She is an inspirational speaker, prophetess, entrepreneur, mentor, playwright, TV host, radio personality, producer and 11x best-selling author, and her overarching mission is to inspire people to fulfill their God-given purpose. Dr. Kishma's work as a speaker and mentor is executed through the Women Destined for Greatness Mentoring Program in Kent County, DE. She believes that despite life's circumstances, there is greatness inside of you! Dr. Kishma A. George is the President and CEO of K.I.S.H. Home, Inc., acronym for Kingdom Investments in Single Hearts (K.I.S.H.) K.I.S.H. Home Inc. was founded out of a desire to impact positively on the lives of girls and women in the state of Delaware as well as those young women who are presently in or have aged out of the foster care system. Dr. George worked as an Independent Living Mentor and witnessed the tremendous challenges that aged-out foster care youth experienced while trying to find their way to a self-sufficient and stable life. A passion within her grew for these young adults and their future as she experienced their frustration in handling basic skills, such as opening a checking/savings account, parenting and the frustration of single parenthood.

Dr. George knew that these young adults, whether they were a single parent or single, needed a strong support system that would empower and encourage them to take control of their lives. They struggled in their transition of leaving foster care because many were still attending high school and were not emotionally or financially stable. After witnessing this, Dr. George began her journey of seeking ways to assist young adults in becoming emotionally and economically self-sufficient so that their transition out of the foster care system and into independent living was successful.

Many of the young adults with whom she worked left the foster care system at 18 years old and found themselves homeless, pregnant, lacking self-esteem, incarcerated, unemployed and without guidance. As a mentor, Dr. George became frustrated by the minimal amount of resources the community offered these young adults. Her dream came to pass and she opened a 24-hour transitional home for young women presently in or recently aged out of the foster care system in Delaware. She makes a difference in their lives and makes certain they have a safe, successful transition to adulthood and independent living.

Her diligence and passion for young women have been recognized in various newspaper articles, including the Dover Post, Delaware News Journal, Delaware State News, and Milford Beacon. She was also featured in the Wisdom for Everyday Life, Kingdom Voices Magazine, Gospel 4 U Magazine, K.I.S.H. Magazine, BOND Inc., and BlogSpot's week spotlight "Fostered Out of Love". In addition, she has appeared as a special guest on the Atlanta LIVE TV Show, Delmarva WBOC- ABC, Life Talk Radio Show with Coach TMB, Live TV Show Straight Talk for Women Only, 101.7 FM Radio, FoxFire Radio Show and The Frank and Travis Radio Show on Praise 105.1. Empowered Women Ministries have recognized Dr. Kishma as Woman of the Year in the category of Entrepreneurial Success, as well as Zeta Phi Beta Sorority, Inc. / Theta Zeta Zeta Chapter for her outstanding involvement in the Greater Dover Community. She was presented with the Diversity Award (2013) from the State of Delaware / Social Services, the Authentic Servant Leadership Award (2014) & New Castle County Chapter of the DSU Alumni Association 33rd annual Scholarship Luncheon for outstanding service to the Wilmington Community and the Delaware State University (2014), Church Girlz Rock; Humanitarian Award (2015), Faith Fighter Award (2016), CHOICES "Woman of the Year" (2016), State of Delaware Office of the Governor Tribute Award (2016), Business Woman of the Year (2016), Global Smashers Award (2017), I AM Baby Doll Global Award (2018), I AM Entrepreneurship Devorah Award (2018) Business Woman of the Year Award (2018) World-Changer Award (2019), I Am Fabulous Award (2019), Phenomenal Woman of the Year (2019), Mogul of the Month (2020). Woman of Influence Spotlight (2020), Phenomenal Woman of the Year (2022) and Leadership & Business Award (2023).

Contact Information:

FB- @kishmageorge

Clubhouse- @kishmageorge

IG- @drkishmageorge

Twitter- @kishmageorge

Tik Tok- @kishmageorge

Website: www.kishmageorge.com

Harness Your Passion

Jacqueline C. Griffith

"The only why to do great work is to love what you do. If you haven't found it yet, keep looking. Don't settle. As with all matters of the heart, you'll know when you find it."
- Steve Jobs

Passion is a powerful emotion that drives us toward our goals and aspirations. It is an intense enthusiasm and excitement fueled by our interests and values. It is an intrinsic motivator that pushes us to do more, improve, and strive for excellence. Passion cannot be taught or learned; it is an instinct from within. It is the unique spark that makes us come alive and feel fulfilled. When we are passionate about something, we are willing to put in the extra effort and time required to succeed.

I started in the childcare industry at nineteen, eager to learn and explore the different aspects of the field. As I gained more experience, I realized that my passion for childcare was not only a job but something I truly enjoyed doing. It was the natural connection that I had with the children that made me realize that childcare was not just a career choice but it was my calling.

My passion for childcare came from my innate desire to make a difference in the lives of young children and their families. I wanted to create an environment where children could thrive, learn, and grow. This passion kept me motivated and helped me overcome the challenges I faced in my career.

One of the biggest challenges I faced as a childcare entrepreneur was finding my unique niche in the industry. With so many players in the field, it was essential to differentiate myself and my services. This is where my passion and creativity came into play. I was determined to bring a fresh perspective to the industry, and I did so by implementing innovative teaching methods and offering a personalized approach to childcare.

Identifying your passion is the first step toward achieving success. Understanding what truly drives you and makes you feel alive is essential. For me, it was the satisfaction of making a positive impact on the lives of young children. If you are struggling to identify your passion, take some time to reflect on the things that make you happy, the activities you enjoy, and the skills that come naturally to you. These can be significant indicators of your passion.

Passion is essential because it gives us a sense of purpose and fulfillment in life. It helps us to identify our unique talents and abilities and to use them to make a positive impact in the world. When we are passionate about something, we are more likely to put in the effort and time required to achieve our goals. We are also more likely to persist in facing obstacles and setbacks.

Passion also leads to increased creativity and innovation. When we are passionate about something, we are more likely to think outside the box, explore new ideas, and come up with innovative solutions. This can lead to discoveries and advancements in various fields.

Passion can also lead to increased happiness and overall well-being. When doing something we truly love, we feel a deep sense of satisfaction and joy. This can help to boost our self-esteem and confidence and to improve our mental and emotional health.

However, pursuing our passion is not always easy. There will be challenges and obstacles along the way, and staying committed and focused on our goals is essential. It is also important to seek support from others, whether friends, family, or a mentor who can offer guidance and motivation when needed.

Identifying your passions is an essential step toward achieving personal fulfillment and success. Your passions are those activities, hobbies, or interests that make you feel alive, happy, and fulfilled. They are the things that you are naturally drawn to and enjoy doing.

Here are some tips for identifying your passions:

Pay attention to what makes you happy: Reflect on the activities that make you feel satisfied and fulfilled. What activities do you enjoy doing in your free time? What hobbies do you have that you are genuinely passionate about? Identifying the things that bring you joy is a great way to discover your passions.

Consider your strengths: What are your natural talents and abilities? What are you good at? Your passions are often closely related to your strengths and skills. Think about the activities that come naturally to you and that you enjoy doing. This can give you some insight into your passions.

Try new things: Sometimes, it takes trying new things to discover your passions. Be open to new experiences and opportunities. Take a class, attend a workshop or volunteer for a cause that interests you. Trying new things can help you discover what you are genuinely passionate about.

Identify your values: Your passions are often closely tied to your values. Think about the important things to you, such as helping others, creativity, or environmental sustainability. These values can help guide you toward your passions.

Ask for feedback: Sometimes, it can be hard to see our passions. Ask your friends and family what they think your passions are. They may be able to offer some insight into what activities or hobbies make you truly happy.

Look for patterns: If you struggle to identify your passions, look for ways in your life. Are there activities or hobbies that you keep coming back to? Do you have a history of being interested in specific topics or activities? Looking for patterns can help you identify your passions.

Pay attention to your emotions. For passions often evoke strong emotions. Think about the activities that excite, energize, or fulfill you. These emotions can be a good indicator of your desires.

Overcoming obstacles and staying committed to your passions is not always easy, but achieving great success and personal fulfillment is essential. Pursuing your desires can be a bumpy road with many challenges and setbacks. However, with dedication and commitment, you can overcome these obstacles and stay true to your passions.

Here are some tips for overcoming obstacles and staying committed to your passions:

Set realistic goals: Setting realistic goals is essential for staying committed to your passions. Break your larger goals into smaller, achievable steps. Celebrate your successes along the way to stay motivated and focused on your ultimate goal.

Embrace failure: Failure is a natural part of the journey toward success. Embrace it as an opportunity to learn and grow rather than a setback. Use your failures to gain new insights and refine your approach toward achieving your goals.

Seek support: Pursuing your passions can be a lonely journey, but it doesn't have to be. Seek help from friends, family, or a mentor who can offer guidance and motivation when needed. Joining a community of like-minded individuals can also be beneficial for staying committed to your passions.

Stay positive: Maintaining a positive attitude is essential for overcoming obstacles and staying committed to your passions. Focus on the progress you have made rather than the setbacks. Keep a positive mindset and remind yourself of why you started pursuing your desires in the first place.

Take care of yourself: Pursuing your passions can be exhausting, both mentally and physically. It's essential to take care of yourself by getting enough rest, eating well, and engaging in self-care activities.

Taking care of yourself will help you stay focused and energized toward achieving your goals.

Stay flexible: Sometimes, your passions may lead you down a different path than you originally intended. Stay relaxed and open to new opportunities and experiences. Embrace change as an opportunity for growth and discovery.

Keep learning: Continuously learning and growing is essential for staying committed to your passions. Stay current on the latest developments in your field and seek opportunities for growth and development.

Many successful individuals have harnessed their passions to achieve great success and personal fulfillment. From entrepreneurs to artists, scientists to athletes, passion has been a driving force behind their success. I am one of those individuals who were fortunate enough to discover my passion for working with young children and use it to achieve my goals and aspirations.

Overcoming obstacles and staying committed to my passion for childcare was not easy, but it was worth it. As a savvy childcare entrepreneur, I have been able to make a positive impact on the lives of countless children and their families. This is something that brings me immense joy and fulfillment.

Pursuing your passions requires dedication, perseverance, and hard work. It also requires a willingness to take risks and embrace failure as a learning opportunity. But it is worth it. When you are doing something that you genuinely love, it brings a sense of purpose and meaning to your life.

If you are struggling to identify your passions, I encourage you to take some time to reflect on the activities that bring you joy and fulfillment. Pay attention to your strengths and abilities, and be open to new experiences and opportunities. Remember that pursuing your passions may not always be easy, but it is worth it in the end.

When you identify your passions and pursue them with dedication and commitment, you can achieve great success and personal fulfillment. You can positively impact the world and leave a lasting legacy. You can inspire others to pursue their passions and achieve their goals.

So, go out there and pursue your passions with all your heart. Don't be afraid to take risks and embrace failure. Stay committed, stay focused, and never give up on your dreams. You will be amazed at what you can achieve when you do this. You will find joy, fulfillment, and personal satisfaction in your work. And most importantly, you will positively impact the world around you.

"Nothing is as important as passion. No matter what you want to do with your life, be passionate."
- Jon Bon Jovi

Jacqueline C. Griffith

Jacqueline has dedicated her life to shaping the lives of youth through providing education and instilling proper guidance. Her innovative curriculum has set the tone in the industry, making her a sought-after educational consultant. As a result, she was featured by The United Teacher Federation, demonstrating the methodology and intricacies of her program's curriculum. Her awareness, wisdom, and ambition have caused a disruption in the childcare industry, which has forged a new path for educators on a national level.

Drawing on three decades of experience, she is proficient in the field of Early Childhood Education, maternal services coordination, childcare directorship and residential counseling, social work, and community/public relations.

Jacqueline is an author, motivational speaker, and coach to both national and international clients in the childcare industry. Her organization, Savvy Child Care Consulting Service, provides entrepreneurs, CEOs, and directors practical solutions to starting and maintaining a childcare business, developing childcare strategies, transforming spaces into childcare environments, setting personal goals, developing essential business techniques, and discovering profitable practices.

Jacqueline's newest endeavor is a children's clothing line and brand called CHILD MOGUL. Her belief is that every child's birthright is to become a "mogul.

Dreaming in the Dark

Dr. Shavona Whitehead

"Pursuing dreams even in a dark season!"

Without explicit permission, I was blessed with a dream much bigger than I could have ever fathomed. It was a dream that I did not seek or pursue. In fact, it came looking for me and found me. It was a dream so big that I could not fully grasp or understand exactly what it meant. Sometimes God will show us what is to come without revealing the steps to get there or the route we should take. Once realized this, I embraced my dream with excitement and exuberance. As it goes with anyone who is happy about something, I shared the greatness of what God had given me with those I loved and trusted. I came to learn that sharing it was one of my greatest downfalls. Where I anticipated and expected love and support, I was met with hatred and abandonment. I even experienced an outright assassination attempt. Something so beautiful was now tainted with the garbage of dismal darkness, and unfortunately, I found myself trapped in a place between Egypt and Exodus.

While I would love to tell you that dealing through the pain of that forsaken place is an isolated incident, I must inform you that the trap I am describing is universal. Seasons of darkness transcend culture, demographics, age, nationality, and gender. Living life in our current day and age will force each of us to endure multiple seasons of darkness. These seasons could include but are not limited to, hardcore bouts with failure, broken relationships, turmoil, grief, rejection, or betrayal. If the truth is told, this list barely scrapes the surface.

When one hears of or thinks about a dark season, it naturally comes with a negative connotation. That concept forces me to wonder: what would happen if we saw our season of darkness as a method of maturation or development? I can already hear you in my spirit. *How can I see the dark season I am in right now as a place of new birth and change? This agony and aggravation are suffocating me. The doubt and desolation are crippling. I am broke, frustrated, and terrified. This feels more like devastation than development.* True. Dark moments can make you feel all of that - and some. We lose ourselves in these feelings and, ultimately, put our destinies at risk because we forget what we already know. Darkness is required before birthing and manifestation can take place.

Before this gets too heavy, I am compelled to remind you here and now that your dark season has a purpose. There is no such thing as time wasted. You will have to shift your perspective if you want to learn how to appreciate how God is using this season to develop you. Your relationship with Him has the potential and power to cause a dramatic shift in the dark. How you embrace this place is poignant preparation for you to walk in the fullness of your dream. This place will shake up what you thought you knew, challenge the strength you possess within, and ignite another level to hold on to what God revealed to you. The time you spend with Him will render you sober about your process. That fresh take on your life will help you determine your next stops while clearly assessing how you will maneuver in these spaces.

Take a quick pause and consider the excursion of someone who is all too familiar with the dark. Think about Joseph. I believe if he took a moment to reflect on his journey, he would tell you that, while it may have been extremely uncomfortable, unfair, and lonely, it developed him for the season that God showed him in his dreams from childhood. That is how it works. Sometimes, God will show us exactly where we are going. Then, more often than not, there are those times when the journey to the destination is a mystery. Either outcome demands and creates a posture that causes us to activate our faith and trust God for the process.

Pure in heart and excited about the wonderful things that God had showed him, Joseph found himself sharing his dreams with those he should have been able to trust and depend on the most, his brothers. He never imagined that these familial pillars would be the very ones to initiate some of the darkest seasons of his life. The toxicity of their jealousy and envy caused them to want to kill him. When they realized how extreme the ramifications of his blood on their hands would be, they decided to sell him into slavery. I have no doubt that Joseph thought his life was over while enduring that place of darkness, but little did he know it was just beginning.

Ask yourself this: *do you have the capacity to believe - even when they refuse to believe in you? Can you believe even when they do everything in their power to rise against you?* Sadly, I know this place all too well. I found myself excited about the anointing that God placed on my life, the call He assigned to my future, and the dream that He revealed to me. I, too, found myself sharing it with the wrong people. While I hate to be the one to share this bad news, I will not let you be ignorant of these facts. Just because people say that they love you and act like they are excited about what God is doing in your life does not always mean they are sincere. The Bible tells us his name was Judas. Today, they are referred to as sister, friend, brother, and confidant.

Those were the people in my life that only wanted to be around me for what they could get out of me. When they wanted me to do things for them and I refused, or if I neglected to respond to them the way they thought I should, the retort was as predictable as the names of the days of the week. A letter under my grandfather's door with a lie to get me in trouble appeared like clockwork. If they chose to not cower behind their pen, they would stop him on his way to his office to lie, just to see his response. I found myself drowning in trouble, all because of what people said about me. I was already held to a high standard because my grandfather always said, *"they will never be able to say I just gave you anything – they will **know** that you earned it."* Yet, they still lied, plotted, and schemed. I was one of the very few that followed the rule because I intentionally wanted to avoid any trouble. Nevertheless, the plots still formed.

What do you do when your dream keeps playing repeatedly in your head, but everything around you contradicts that dream? I am happy to tell you and it is simple, never change your posture while you are in the dark because greatness is developed there. The full picture does not become clear until it goes into the darkroom. The image must be positioned, submerged, tested, and developed before it comes forth. And the photographer can be sure that the images they saw in his camera will be produced with clarity and color - once the process is done.

Once sold into slavery, favor followed Joseph. Why? The favor of God on his life was implicitly embedded in his DNA, not in the coat that was violently and viciously taken from him. Even while serving in Potiphar's house, he was incarcerated and yet still favored. Not willing to compromise and jeopardize his God-given protection, provision, and position - because that is what favor is – Joseph found himself being lied on, which ultimately landed him in jail. While imprisoned on false charges, in a situation where many of us would lose hope, Joseph never forgot his dream. God showed up for him and favor followed him. I can almost hear him saying *my gift and anointing showed up even in the place of oppression, so I still knew my dream would manifest.*

When you are favored by God and there is a promise on your life, there is no situation or circumstance that can terminate your ultimate destination. You will reach the point of your promise at the appointed time. You must believe even when it seems as though all is being snatched away from you and everyone is against you. This was a life lesson I learned for myself. I was discouraged, but there was no point in lying dormant in that place. I knew there was too much greatness in me to allow the naysayers to stop me. It was God that called me, not the people that were against me. Their plots may have knocked me off of the perch God built, but they never stopped me from working, producing, and manifesting. What they thought would be my downfall was really my much-needed time in the birth chamber. God was using the dark moments to develop me; all I had to do was push my way through.

My dark season made me question the totality of my value and worth. I was in an unfamiliar place that caused me to lose focus on my promise. I retreated. The loneliness that came with that part of my journey made me feel like I was no longer good enough for the promise. However, I came to realize something. I thought I was simply lying around and wasting away in the dark, but in reality, God was forcing me to take the time to acknowledge just how carefully He was illuminating my dream. I was captive in the dark place – and He was still molding, making, and transforming me for the dream. I could not find my way out of the dismal and deadly darkness, but I was safe. God was teaching me that the only way out, over, or through was Him. And I had to give Him my complete confidence. Shavona's strength was a feeble and unavailable option. God's strength was the only solution.

I hope you do not mind, but I would like to have a very real honest and open moment. When God gives you a dream, that dream will always be bigger than you and go beyond what you can do alone. It may not even make sense; however, it is a dream full of power and purpose. I remember God showing me the work He was assigning to my hands. The moment I committed myself to working through the vision, every possible obstacle made itself known. It went well beyond the persecution of people and the betrayal of others. Out of nowhere, my finances seemed non-existent. Everything I encountered and frankly needed came with an astronomical fee, and I did not have the personal finances to meet the need. Yet, every time I told myself I could not do it and that it would be impossible, God decided to reveal even more of the dream to me.

Even with the glimmer of light, He was trying to show me, I kept falling into a deeper and darker hole. When I looked up to assess just how bad it really was, I saw that I eventually began struggling with not feeling adequate to fulfill the task He had given me. I felt as though I had been indefinitely abandoned by those who I thought would cover and support me. I could see the dream clear as day, right in front of me, but I was unable to financially start or sustain it. *How can this really be my dream if I am incapable of doing the work that will make it come true?* Yes, this is the question that I asked myself. *God, did you really call me to do this?* It was at that moment that I had to shift my thinking. Yes, God gave me the dream, but this was His dream. I was merely the vessel that had to muster up the gull and grace to speak to the dream. I had to believe in it, pray over it, and most importantly, protect it at all costs.

Let me be very clear: the presentation of your posture matters while you are in the dark! So do your verbiage, your thoughts, and your movements. Your words can be the lifeboat that gets you over or the iceberg that sinks the ship. You must speak the language of where you are going, not where you are. Watch what you say in the dark. Language strengthens your posture to handle the dark season well. Your mentality will make all the difference. Just like the Bible says, as a man thinks, so is he. And being in the proper position is key. When God says move, MOVE! Your posture should have you ready at any moment to freely shift to wherever God is taking you. Too often, we allow where we are to dictate how we will respond.

When you have a dream, you must believe it even when you are the only one that can see it.

Tell yourself right now, I can maintain my dream in the dark. We lose sight of the fact that there is purpose in anything God allows into our situation. The dark season was not created for your demise. On the contrary, that space was specifically curated for your good. You cannot stop making moves just because you are in a dark season of your life that has temporarily made the dream seem impossible. There is still very substantial work to be done in this season, no matter how uncomfortable or uncertain. Your current surroundings cannot fully compress your belief. You must keep dreaming in the dark.

Traveling the path back to the light will take endurance and perseverance. Do not be deceived. There will be many times when giving up, or staying in the dark, will look like the most sensible option. Here is where you must adjust your own perspective. You must learn to see the blessings that come along the way. God will send you help in the dark season. Rest assured, that is not a thought or a concept. I know it to be a fact. Do not miss your access to the countless resources that have been provided to you, even if you received them in the dark. We often delay our own process because those resources do not necessarily come the way we think they should. If Joseph had allowed his present state to delay his promise, he would have stayed in the dark much longer than needed. But because he operated in his faith, he got help from some of the least likely places. He was sent to Potiphar - help. He was turned over to the jailers – help. Pharaoh sent for him because of his gift -

help. Joseph saw his help, received it accordingly, and never stopped operating in his gift or anointing.

That dedication to God's plan for his life changed everything. The dreamer became the interpreter of dreams. On top of favor, Joseph now had a reputation that preceded him. His name was being spoken in rooms where his feet had never touched the floor by people he did not know. You will learn, through trial and error, that you must stand firm on your dream. Because God trusted you with it, He will be the one to ensure that provision is made for the dream. Are you wondering how I know? I came to appreciate that, even in my dark season, people were having conversations about me. Yes, I know. It is a hard pill to swallow. People I had never met were discussing my anointing and my gift. These conversations manifested the dream that God had already given me. And because I maintained my posture, oil, anointing and composure during the bondage, darkness, oppression and despair, God blessed me with double.

Just like Joseph, I can say with assurance that I have this profound testimony: my posture propelled me into destiny. Acknowledge the fact our suffering is often done in the spotlight. So, it matters how you go through your dark seasons. When Joseph's dream came to pass, the ones that so desperately sought his demise found themselves at his mercy. It is rather interesting that when they found themselves before him, they did not even recognize him. I find it amazing that the ones who once said they loved and cared for you can turn around, set out to kill and destroy you, and then not recognize you when the dream they said was impossible comes to pass. I had to realize that I was no longer the person they knew when they left for dead in the place that we were. My dream had come to fruition, and my identity was forever changed.

Throughout his journey, Joseph never let go of the fact that he was still the dreamer. He knew the dream that God gave him and trusted it, no matter what season of the journey he was experiencing. If you are going to see and walk in the promise of your dream, you must be committed to the journey, no matter how it looks. It will never be about who you know; it will always be about what you know. You know exactly what God has spoken to you. Never doubt what you know simply because your sight contradicts your spirit. In truth, Joseph teaches us a powerful lesson. When they came before him, although he now had the power to condemn them, he gently revealed his true identity. He made one solid statement: *You meant it for evil, but God meant it for my good!* Joseph had already forgiven them because he knew that God's hand rested on his life and that the dark season prepared him for the moment of prosperity, power, and authority in which he was now able to walk.

This was a key component to me embracing the fullness of my own dream. I had to forgive those that never wanted to see me survive - not for them, but for me. Your dream is way too powerful for you to allow unforgiveness to hinder you. During the darkness of the in-between, I learned so much about me. I began to see myself in God like I never had prior to the darkness. I leaned in and embraced the woman God called, chose, and anointed with His dream.

Even after all they tried, God still had me in mind because of purpose. I wrestled with being stuck in bondage, but He still had me in mind. I was fastened to a lock and key but still operating in power while He had me in mind. Joseph's pit, prison and palace experience opened my eyes to how real God can be. I cannot despise my own rise out of the darkness because it prepared me for what was next. I learned to see each part of the darkness as a necessary part of the birthing of my dream. My pit gave me the tenacity to keep pushing. My prison taught me the strategy to manifest the dream. And my palace experience not only reminded me of God's favor, but also proved to be the dwelling place of my dream.

Dreamer, let me encourage you. In between the giving of the dream and the manifestation of that same dream, God will take you through training exercises that will teach you some valuable lessons and developmental processes while you endure through the dark seasons. Your posture matters during these moments. Can you see God's purpose even when the light refuses to shine on it? Can you still see and believe in your dream when it seems like everything contradicts what you saw? Can you trust God enough, even in the dark, to still walk forward not knowing where the end of the tunnel will lead? Consider it – dreaming comes at a cost.

God equipped you to carry His dream; therefore, He will not only guide you through the process, but He will also provide provision for the dream. The greatest work that God performs is in the dark. Lean in, trust Him with everything in you, and posture yourself for the appointed time so that the dream can manifest. The way has already been prepared for you. It may get uncomfortable, feel inconvenient, seem impossible, and look like the dream was fake. That is the moment that you must believe God all the more. Your dark season is not time wasted; it is a time full of purpose, development, and strengthening. Can you keep dreaming in the dark? Yes, you can because the dream shall manifest! You were built for this, dreamer. Ignite and embrace your dream!

Dr. Shavona's Acknowledgements

First, I must honor and praise God for choosing me. I am so grateful to be God's Girl and to walk out the footsteps that HE ordained and established for me. I'm not worthy, but I am grateful. I vow to honor God with every fiber of my being.

I honor and celebrate the legacy of my angels, my grandparents, Walter, and Irma Bronson. I am the woman I am today because of what they instilled and invested in me. To my mom and best friend, Iris, thank you for believing in me and pushing me to go after my dreams no matter what. To my aunt Winona, thank you for being my listening ear, confidant, and my inspiration.

Special thanks to my husband, Yusef, who supported me even when he didn't understand my dreams and the vision God gave me. To my amazing Butterflies, my mentees, it is you that became the evidence of the manifestation of the dream just like God showed me. My oil and the weight that I carry is heavy, but it is so worth it when I get to watch you embrace your journeys even when you must dream in the dark.

To my MORE Experience community, thank you for taking this journey with me. As I always say, "My Journey Is Someone's Freedom," and it's my honor to share it with you. To my family and friends, thank you for your push, love, and support.

Dr. Shavona Whitehead

DR. SHAVONA L. WHITEHEAD, BS, MDIV, DMIN

A trailblazer in ministry, Dr. Shavona Whitehead has been anointed to plant, grow and shape various ministries worldwide. She began her journey in May of 2006, being ordained as an elder in the Pentecostal faith. As Dr. Von continued to seek God, she transitioned in March 2009 to the Baptist denomination under the power and wisdom of her beloved grandfather and spiritual father, the late Rev. Dr. Walter Bronson Jr. It was under his nurturing that her spiritual gifts were developed. As she continued to seek God for her purpose and calling, her prophetic training flowed under Bishop Christopher Windley.

Dr. Whitehead's goal has always been to fulfill the will of God outlined in her life by spreading the gospel of Jesus Christ across the nations. While teaching others about Christ, she has made her mission to teach and help women to turn their ashes into beauty, increasing their self-esteem, thus cultivating spiritual growth and becoming great women of wisdom and integrity. She believes and teaches women that they must seek the Lord to find out how they can become more. In 2020, Dr. Whitehead launched "She's More Now" Life and Empowerment Coaching. MORE stands for Motivated Overcomers being Restored and Empowered. Within this platform, women learn that they are MORE when God speaks even while he is manifesting it.

As her purpose continues to unfold, Dr. Whitehead launched Dr. Shavona Whitehead, LLC, under which Manifesting MORE with Dr. Von, Break The Box Cohort and The ROAR Experience (Restore Overcome Affirm and Release) were incorporated. As The MORE Pusher, she creates rooms and experiences where women can experience a wholistic healing that ignites wholeness.

Dr. Whitehead has taken her place in Christ in the world but has also diligently gained her education. After receiving her education from the Baltimore City School System, she got a Bachelor of Science degree in Management Science from Coppin State University and her Master of Divinity from Wesley Theological Seminary. She holds her Doctor of Ministry Degree in Social & Environmental Justice from the Interdenominational Theological Center & Morehouse School of Religion in Atlanta, Ga. She is trained in Spiritual Chaplaincy through the Johns Hopkins Hospital Department of Spiritual Care and Chaplaincy Internship Program and is a certified life coach.

Dr. Whitehead is the published author of "I Am More Now Empowerment Journal" and her most recent book "The Cutting that Made me Whole, "as well as being a contributing author on many best-seller-acclaimed bodies of work. She has continuously soared above her pain and circumstances to continue to be more through all she has gone through. She has been featured in many digital network publications, illuminated on Atlanta billboards, featured on major radio, television, and newspaper outlets. Dr. Whitehead is also an Executive Producer with the Women Win Network. Dr. Whitehead has the support of her husband, four children, and many of those who have flourished under her leadership.

Contact Information for Dr. Shavona L. Whitehead

"The MORE Pusher"

Website – www.shavonawhitehead.com

Email: info@shavonawhitehead.com

Facebook – Shavona Whitehead

Facebook – The MORE Experience

Instagram - @IAmDrVon

YouTube – Dr. Shavona Whitehead

LinkedIn – Dr. Shavona Whitehead

I Dare to Dream

Simra Dalmida

Are you someone who often daydreams about the possibilities and potential of life? Do you strongly desire to pursue your passions and make your wildest dreams a reality? If so, then you are likely a dreamer at heart, with a creative and imaginative spirit that is just waiting to be unleashed.

Being a dreamer can be both a blessing and a curse, as you may often find yourself lost in thought or struggling to stay focused on the tasks at hand. However, it is important to remember that your dreams and aspirations make you unique and set you apart from others. To embrace the dreamer in you, here are some tips to help you stay motivated and inspired:

- Write your goals and dreams, and break them down into smaller, achievable steps.

- Surround yourself with like-minded individuals who support and encourage your vision.

- Take risks and don't be afraid to fail, as failure is often a valuable learning experience.

- Practice self-care and take time to recharge your creative energy.
- Believe in yourself and your abilities, and don't let anyone else's doubts or negativity hold you back.

Remember, the world needs dreamers like you to imagine and create a better future. So, keep dreaming big and pursuing your passions because anything is possible with determination and hard work.

My Reflection

Looking back at my own experiences, I recall a time when I would gaze at the mountain top and plead with God to take me away from my birthplace, the Virgin Islands, because of the pain it had caused me. I wasn't fully committed to God and was living in a backslidden state. But God never gave up on me. I experienced unnecessary pain and delay because I was living life on my terms and failed to understand my purpose in life. I was chasing after my own dreams instead of following the divine purpose God had for me. Due to my disobedience, I went down many roads and encountered so many delays because of not obeying God. At the age of 34, my life changed for good. The transformation took place, and I finally understood what it meant to have an intimate relationship with Jesus Christ.

From Tragedy to Triumph: My Profound Spiritual Awakening

Through my journey of loss and grief, I learned that spirituality can be a powerful tool in coping with tough times. The experience of losing loved ones is always a difficult one, but my faith helped me find the strength to move forward. I realized that my profound spiritual awakening was an important turning point in my life, and it allowed me to focus on what really matters.

As I continued to grow spiritually, I noticed that I became more aware of the world around me. I was able to appreciate the beauty in everything and everyone, and I found myself feeling more compassionate towards others. This newfound awareness helped me to see the visions that God had gifted me with, giving me the courage and strength to pursue my goals.

Through my faith, I achieved my dreams of attaining a bachelor's degree, getting engaged, and marrying the love of my life. My spiritual awakening also allowed me to recognize the signs that led me to my husband and son. I truly believe that God has a plan for all of us, and through my faith, I could see the path He had laid out for me.

My journey has taught me that no matter what life throws your way, you can always find solace and strength in your faith. I am grateful for my spiritual awakening and the impact it has had on my life.

Divine Dreams: Trusting in God's Timing

God has blessed me with numerous dreams that initially seemed unattainable. For instance, I never thought I was worthy of marriage, but in 2014, my dream of finding a husband came true. Additionally, God revealed to me that I would have a son, and in 2016, my son was born. Praise be to God! Not only did He bless me with a son, but also a daughter for my husband. I was able to move from living on an income base to a suburban lifestyle, all thanks to Him. However, it didn't happen overnight – everything was in His timing. Trusting in God has allowed me to fulfill my dreams beyond what I thought was possible.

The Power of Trusting God's Plan: Pursuing Dreams and Visions with Faith

I can still remember holding Bible study in my home before I got married and feeling God's presence as He revealed to me a vision of a store and women. At the time, I wasn't quite sure what He meant, and being a baby in Christ, I couldn't fully grasp the significance of His message. Yet over the years, I learned that when He gives you a dream or vision, it's important to trust Him completely. Sometimes, it may take years before the vision comes to fruition - in my case, it took 13 years. But God's timing is always perfect. That's why it's crucial to document everything that He reveals to you because I am living proof that it will come to pass.

I recall my sister in Christ telling me that I have a book inside of me, and while I shrugged it off initially, I now realize that our life is indeed a book, a powerful testimony to God's glory. Fast forward to 2023, after three years of pandemic, and God has not forgotten the dream that He gave me. In 2022, He made it happen - my online boutique finally became a brick-and-mortar store, despite the odds. I was awed by His suddenness and faithfulness.

Entering 2023, God spoke to me again, reminding me to expand just when I thought I had reached my limit. I had questions, of course - how was I going to afford this? Was it too fast? But God knew my concerns even before I voiced them. I went through negotiations and told God that I would know if it was His will or not when they came back with a denial. But they didn't - they came back with a resounding yes and much more than I expected. I know now that it was all God, not me.

So, I encourage you to keep dreaming, keep pressing forward, and keep trusting in His plan. It may take time, and there may be challenges along the way, but never doubt that God is faithful to His promises. I dare to dream because I know that He is speaking to me in my dreams and visions.

A Reminder to Trust in Your Dreams and Choose Your Confidants Carefully

It's important to remember that not everyone will believe or understand the message that God is sending you, especially with the dreams He's given you. Be cautious of who you share your aspirations with, as not everyone can handle it. The Bible offers us a prime example of this with Joseph and his brothers. They couldn't accept the visions that God presented to Joseph and became envious and resentful.

Given the sensitive nature of sharing one's aspirations, it's crucial to be discerning about who you choose to confide in. Not everyone will share your vision or understand the message that God is sending you, and that's okay. It's important to remember that you don't need validation from others to pursue your God-given dreams. However, seeking wise counsel from trusted friends and mentors who can offer constructive feedback and support is also important.

Joseph's story in the Bible is a powerful reminder that not everyone will be receptive to our dreams and aspirations. His brothers couldn't accept the visions that God had given Joseph and allowed jealousy and resentment to take hold. But Joseph remained faithful to God's plan for his life, even in the face of adversity.

As you pursue your own dreams, remember to stay grounded in your faith and seek guidance from those who share your values and beliefs. Surround yourself with people who will uplift and encourage you, and don't be discouraged by those who may not understand your journey. With God's guidance and the support of a strong community, you can achieve great things.

Let's take a moment to reflect on Joseph's story from the Bible.

Joseph, a dreamer, shared his visions with his brothers, including one where he and his siblings were depicted as sheaves of wheat. Joseph didn't realize how his excitement would affect his brothers. This dream angered his brothers so much that they plotted to kill him. Instead, they ended up selling him into slavery. This story is relevant today because we must be careful who we trust with our dreams. It's important to note that pursuing our dreams is not always easy. We may face criticism, rejection, or even failure along the way. However, it's important to remember that setbacks and challenges are a normal part of the journey. We can learn from our mistakes and use them as opportunities to grow and improve.

Another important lesson we can learn from Joseph's story is the power of forgiveness. Despite being betrayed and mistreated by his own brothers, Joseph was able to forgive them and reconcile with them. This act of forgiveness not only brought Joseph peace but also brought healing to his family.

As we pursue our dreams, we may encounter people who hurt us or let us down. It's important to remember that holding onto anger and resentment will only hold us back. By choosing to forgive and let go of the past, we can free ourselves from the burden of anger and move forward towards our goals with a clear mind and heart.

Closing Remarks

Dreams are a powerful tool that can give us insight into our own thoughts and emotions. They can also provide guidance and direction when we are feeling lost or uncertain. When we pay attention to our dreams and document them, we open ourselves up to a world of possibilities. We can use our dreams to inspire, motivate, and guide us towards our goals.

God is always speaking to us, and sometimes he chooses to do so through our dreams. When we are faithful and obedient, he will reveal his plans for us in ways that we can understand. It is important to trust in his timing and to have patience, even when things seem uncertain. Remember, he is the God who makes the impossible possible and will always provide the resources we need to fulfill his plans for our lives.

So, keep dreaming, keep writing, and don't be afraid to take risks. God has given each of us unique talents and gifts, and he wants us to use them to positively impact the world. When we dare to dream and step out in faith, we can accomplish amazing things. So go ahead, dream big, and get ready to be astounded by what God can do through you. Dare to Dream!

An Important Message for my Readers:

Remember to Dream Big!

Here are some additional thoughts to keep in mind as you pursue your dreams:

- It's important to have a clear idea of what you want to achieve but be open to unexpected opportunities and paths that may lead you to your goal.

- Surround yourself with people who support and encourage your dreams. They can provide valuable feedback and help you stay motivated.

- Remember that setbacks and failures are a natural part of the process. Use them as learning experiences and don't let them discourage you from pursuing your dreams.

- Celebrate your successes, no matter how small they may seem. Acknowledge the progress you've made and use it to fuel your continued efforts.

- Finally, don't forget to enjoy the journey. Pursuing your dreams can be challenging, but it can also be incredibly rewarding and fulfilling. Enjoy the process and savor the moments along the way. Dare to Dream!!

Simra's Acknowledgement and Gratitude

I would like to extend my heartfelt gratitude and appreciation to my Heavenly Father, Jesus Christ, for His guidance through the Holy Spirit. Without Him, embarking on this journey would have been impossible. I also want to express my love and thanks to my wonderful husband, Richard Dalmida, and my children Devontea, Daiheem, Sa'miya, Rachel and Ephraim for their unwavering love and support.

I am deeply grateful to my mentor and friend, Dr. Kishma George, whose visionary guidance, and belief in me made this endeavor possible. Thank you for helping me pursue what God has purposed for my life, for His Glory.

I would also like to thank my Auntie, Greta, and best friend, Tiffany, for their prayerful support and for believing in the dream that God has placed inside of me. You are my cheerleaders in both the spiritual and natural world.

To my spiritual parents and my church family at The Potter's House International Ministries, thank you for your unwavering support and encouragement. I am blessed to have you all in my life.

Lastly, I want to thank my mom and dad, who have always believed in me. Your love and support mean everything to me.

To my readers, remember that it's okay to dream and to write out your vision. Even if it takes some time, it will surely come to pass. **Dream big and never give up!**

Coach Simra Dalmida

Author/ Speaker/Coach/Business Owner/ Wife / Mother of five is the many hats that Simra wears. A native of St. Thomas U.S. Virgin Islands, born on December 7th, 1976, to the parents of Carlitos and Sonia Grant. Simra is a living example of how God can transform a life to help others. She has been through many obstacles from childhood to adulthood and by the grace of God, she is still here to tell her story. Only upon surrendering her life to Christ did God begin to unveil the purpose for which He had called her.

She is now the proud Founder and CEO of Empowering Woman 4 Excellence Coaching and Stepping into My Destiny Shoe Boutique LLC. Simra graduated from the University of Phoenix with a B.S. in Healthcare Administration and Liberty University, where she obtained her two master's degrees, one in Human Services/Life Coaching and the other in Interdisciplinary Studies /Life Coaching.

Armed with several degrees, business, healing, and a new perspective on life. Simra no longer allowed pain to dictate her life and soon realized that, during it all, God was positioning her to pursue her greatest passion: empowering and equipping women to live on purpose.

Simra feels honored that God strategically selected her to empower, edify, and educate women. Her testimony reminds women that they can overcome every obstacle and, more importantly, turn their pain into purpose and impact lives worldwide.

The Dreamer In You

Tiffany McCullough

When considering the phrase, '*The Dreamer in You*,' one is inspired to examine their own innermost desires. This gives us the impression that there is something inside that requires great incision. When a surgeon considers a surgical procedure, the end result is carefully examined to ensure safety and proper outcome of the intended outcome. Therefore, the term incision is used because the surgeon carefully considers how the procedure will bring the end results. It's important to understand that God releases His passion and will upon you when you have a dream. According to the dictionary, a dream is a series of sensations, images, and thoughts that occur in a person's mind while they sleep. Moreover, it is regarded as an ideal or aspiration.

How does a child grow up to accomplish or become what they dreamed of in their youth? As a preschool teacher, hearing children discuss what they want to be when they grow up encourages me to see them as that. When hearing the shouts of laughter along the erase boards of time, the days illuminated with the passions of each child's heart. I aspire to see each child dream and believe. I enjoy hearing the excitement of their echoes: *I want to be a doctor! I want to be a firefighter! I want to be a lawyer! I want to be the President of the United States of America!* It brings my heart so much joy and tranquility to know that these children will someday become their dreams.

As for you, the reader, I encourage your heart to hear what Heavenly Father has released upon each page. Dreams are given by God for a variety of reasons and purposes. Having dreams is very important to fulfilling God's purpose and plan on earth. You should never doubt what you believe God for or what He has shown you; it is not irrelevant. The dreamer in you must come forth in Jesus Christ's mighty Name! Therefore, I believe it was intended for you to read this book.

> *"For I know the thoughts that I think towards you, saith the Lord, thoughts of peace, and not of evil, to give you an expected end."*
> *- Jeremiah 29:11*

When considering the phrase 'expected end,' the word 'incision' comes to mind. Christ has already planned your future and destiny, but many of us take detours that necessitate the incision of our dreams. Incisions of our dreams refer to those things the Father must remove that unlawfully attached themselves to our divine purpose and destiny. When you think about a leech, what comes to mind? A leech is a bloodsucking parasite, an aquatic or terrestrial annelid worm with suckers at both ends. Now, let's consider the spiritual realm. The enemy often sends spiritual leeches to feed off of the hard-working majority. These leeches prey on others or extort profit from them.

A leech clings to another for personal gain, especially without giving anything in return. So here's what I want you to do: be your own surgeon. For you to unleash the dreamer within you, you must rid yourself of the leeches that have been draining you and preventing you from being your best self.

One of the things I love about God is that He doesn't renege on His promises. We are born into who we are supposed to be. The Scriptures tell us that we are predestined from our mother's womb.

"Before I made you in your mother's womb, I chose you. Before you were born, I set you apart for a special work. I appointed you as a prophet to the nations."
- Jeremiah 1:5

In this passage, we see how God appointed Jeremiah "as a prophet to the nations." When we think about nations, we typically consider them to be something large and vast, beyond human control. We understand that God's appointment for Jeremiah may have been intimidating and fearful; Jeremiah may have experienced many consuming emotions. When looking at himself in the flesh, Jeremiah said to the Lord, "*I do not know how to speak; I am only a child*" (Jeremiah 1:6). In this scenario, Jeremiah is essentially saying, "Lord, don't you remember that I have a disability that makes me incompetent to do what You're asking of me? I have a speech problem that reminds me of my frailty and inability to stand, except You go before and with me." Despite Jeremiah's inadequacies, the Lord reminded him of who He is. Likewise, the Lord is telling us that He knew us before we were ever conceived or thought of by man. Therefore, nothing is a secret to God.

We must remember God's truth when we examine our lives, especially when we feel discouraged or inadequate. In the eyes of God, we are always valuable and He has a purpose for our lives. If God puts a dream in you, He will provide all that you need. And no weapon that is formed against you shall be able to prosper! The dreamer in you shall come forth! I see a stirring of the waters in your belly as these writings are scribed upon the tablets of your heart. The dreamer in you shall come forth!

God sends dreams to instruct, reveal His will, warn against evil, and answer our prayers, among other reasons. Therefore, God will bypass our intellect (our reasoning or understanding) to communicate to our soul through dreams. Why does God communicate this way? The Father operated in space and time in ways that would later be interpreted and inscripturated by Moses. During the time when God began explaining the gospel of salvation to Abraham, the Bible did not exist. When God places a dream within us, He endows us with special revelation to accomplish the purposes of redemption.

Whenever God gave His people a dream, it was for a divine purpose. The Bible illustrates this truth in various stories. In Genesis 37, Joseph had multiple dreams that foretold his rise to power. In Genesis 41, Joseph interpreted the dreams of Pharaoh. In Genesis 28, God met Jacob in a dream, which revealed His presence in the land of Canaan. In Genesis 20, God protected Abimelech, King of Gerar, from sleeping with Abraham's wife, Sarah, by means of a dream. As depicted in these texts, God appeared to each person in a dream. Likewise, what is God showing you? What is it that you're believing God for? The dreams that God desires for us to pursue are the ones that are aligned with truth and His perfect will.

> *"For God speaketh once, yea twice, yet man perceive it not. God speaks to man in dreams and visions, delivering those cast into the pit and restores life.*
> *- Job 33:14-15*

It is the Father's passion that you fulfill your purpose in life; His passion has placed the dreamer in you! And that dream calls out from within until one tires of searching for fulfillment outside of God's will. The dream beckons and speaks to one's soul until the spirit of man is relinquished in the presence of the Almighty God. Every aspect of your being is infused with the dreamer within you, until heart to heart and toe to toe; you yield to who the Father has placed you on earth to be. Alignment paints the sketches of your destiny and lodges you into your future. The dreamer in you must come into full agreement with the Father's will.

Change Your Frequency

When we talk about frequency and dreams, it's literally the linking of vibrations. It's a person's emotional state or atmosphere within a place, and/or the associations of an object as communicated to and felt by others. When we take a close look at the connection the two have, we find that frequency and vibration are of importance to one another. An individual's vibration is their mental and emotional state of being. So when it's high, you'll feel more confident and in touch with yourself. Taking a look at 2 Corinthians 3:18, we see that it deals with frequency:

> *"And we all, with unveiled faces, beholding the glory of*
> *the Lord, are being transformed*
> *into the same image from one degree of glory to another.*
> *For this comes*
> *from the Lord who is the spirit."*
> *-2 Corinthians 3:18*

As we look at this Scripture verse in part, we transform into the same image from one degree of glory to another. This speaks of levels, change, elevation, and transformation. I believe this is where frequency and vibration meet to coexist as two units that already existed before the beginning of time. Again, this goes back to the Scripture that tells us, "I knew you before you were born or ever conceived in your mother's womb" (Jeremiah 1:5). The dreamer in you was already there when God breathed on you the breath of life; you just had to come into it. What you must understand is that there is a sound that gives birth to dreams. When you align with God's Word, purpose, and vision, you are releasing a sound that vibrates heaven, releasing what is yours.

When Moses came down from Mount Sinai with the Ten Commandments, his face glowed from being in God's presence (2 Corinthians 3:13-18). Whenever your dreams come into agreement with Heaven, something happens. The airwaves send signals that the dreamer in you lives. It is the frequency that allows you to connect and vibrate in the divine energy of the Heavenly Father. It is a very high energy frequency and the highest frequency in the angelic realms. This represents unity – oneness with purpose and vision.

"I appeal to you, dear brothers and sisters, by the authority of our Lord Jesus Christ, to live in harmony with each other. Let there be no divisions in the church. Rather, be of one mind, united in thought and purpose."
- 1 Corinthians 1:10

Arise and Anoint Him

Arise! This is a bold statement that indicates action or the emergence of something new. It's like visualizing a rose that emerges from the dirt and blooms into what it was intended to be. As I look at each of our lives, we all have a particular path we must travel in order to become. It is inspiring to see the life of David, as well as the lives of many other men and women of God.

After David was anointed to become the next king, he didn't know the Goliaths he would have to face. Yet, his love for God allowed him to walk out the dreamer within him. Life experiences and challenges are what assist with the birth of who we are. I look at these as life pains or unwanted moments of test, heartache, and/or persecution. Whenever we stand in the moment of a challenging season, life may dictate to us that we have reached our limit, our dreams have died, and that we have no strength to carry on. But as we change our frequency, our vibration enacts heaven to respond to its own.

> *But we are citizens of heaven, where the Lord Jesus Christ lives. And we are eagerly waiting for him to return as our savior.*
> *- Philippians 3:20*

Let's look at the moment David walked through the door–possibly sweaty, dirty, and tired from tending to the sheep. He was anointed king at that moment, but it was in secret. David was not publicly anointed until much later (2 Samuel 2:4, 5:3). Saul was still legally the king, but God was preparing David for his future responsibilities. Each king and priest was anointed with oil; this commissioned him as God's representative. As such, hear this, the dreamer in you has been called out, hand-picked, and chosen by God. You must understand that the dream God has given you and every vision the Father has shown you is intended to bring glory to His name. So, you must walk out your dreams. The passion that God has placed down on the inside of you that keeps calling and pulling on you is God's calling on your life. God chooses you for this dream. Among all David's brothers, God called David from the field where he was tending sheep.

God already had David on his mind, just like He had you on His mind before you were ever conceived. God supernaturally gifts you with what you need to fulfill the dreamer in you. David not only killed a lion and a bear with his own hands, but he also took down a great warrior with only a slingshot. If we can be real, most of us probably would have ran or hid just like the other soldiers. Nevertheless, there are some who trust God and are willing to face the Goliaths in their lives that try to prevent them from reaching their destiny. There's a particular passage that sticks out to me.

> *"A gift opens the way and ushers the giver into the presence of the great."*
> *- Proverbs 18:16*

When we are gifted with the dream, God allows a season of sensing great expectations from within and around us (1 Samuel 16:18, 17:34-37). There will be trials to test your dream.

"Because you know the testing of your faith produces perseverance."
- James 1:3

As you journey towards your dreams, you must believe that God will provide everything you need. David had to learn how to navigate treacherous territory; the Lord always provided a hiding place for him. God will give you direction concerning your dream.

*"I will instruct you and teach you in the way you should go; I will counsel you
with my loving eye on you."*
- Psalm 32:8

As you trust '*The Dreamer in You*,' God will guide you, and you will be able to navigate your journey knowing where to hide and who to trust. The Lord always guided David to where he needed to be. We must grow to trust God in the dark places in our lives when the dreamer in us appears to be dormant and quiet. When the dream does not speak but gives you utter silence, that's when you re-channel your frequency until you get the right signal that says *connection*!

Tiffany's Acknowledgments

I would like to take the time to say Thank you to my good friend and sister, Crystal Love. I'm grateful for the friendship we have and the decades of sisterhood God has allowed us to share.

I also want to thank God for each one of my children, Devontae, Da'montae, Emmanuel, and Colin. As a mother with sons, I thank God He chose me to Love, nurture, teach, and guide each of you. I love you all very much; you inspire me to push beyond limits. Mommy!

Tiffany McCullough

Tiffany McCullough is the founder of A New Revelation World Outreach Inc., a nonprofit organization that assists youth and their parents by offering programs that target deep-rooted issues. These programs establish a structure within the family home environment, communities, and schools. She is also the owner of Early Readers Family Fun Childcare.

Tiffany studied at FAM Institute Bible College & Seminary in Baltimore, MD. She is a licensed minister, certified counselor, and licensed childcare provider. She is currently pursuing her PhD in Christian Counseling. In addition, she effectively demonstrates hope through her playwrights, book writings, newsletters, and other works of art.

She has written, performed, and produced various plays, such as: Rain Down, He Is Risen, Another Chance, Rock-A-By-Baby, and many others that have captivated audiences with tears, laughter, and thoughts of reflection.

As a native of Baltimore, MD, Tiffany McCullough has served as an advocate and an activist for family empowerment. She has served in various capacities by dedicating her life to helping inner city youth and their families as she strives to change the projection and stigma of divorce.

I Am The Dream Walking

By: Dr. Nephetina L. Serrano

The esteemed Queen Nefertiti was a royal of the 18th Dynasty of Ancient Egypt and, with her husband, reigned during what was arguably the wealthiest period of Ancient Egyptian history. She was known as The Queen of Love. A goddess in her own right, she would one day rule as Pharaoh herself. She was made famous by her bust, which resided in a Berlin museum, being one of the most copied works of Ancient Egypt. As a girl, I always remembered her golden silhouette illustrated across encyclopedia pages and fashioned on the golden bamboo earrings and pendants dangling around the ears and necks of American youth in the 80s. A side profile always displayed Nefertiti's stately crown in place, her chin to the sky in pride; she was venerated as the epitome of regal splendor. My name, Nephetina, although sounding phonetically much like the former, had a unique ending, indicating a variation of meaning: *"beautiful beloved companion,"* making me a unique goddess in my own right. However, it took overcoming and enduring many of life's ups and downs, victories and hardships, to now be able to hold my head up high like that well-known bust.

I'm a native of Philadelphia, Pennsylvania, where I was born and raised. My mother had me at the tender age of seventeen, so naturally, we lived with my grandparents for most of my early elementary years in an area of the city referred to as West Philly. Growing up with my grandmother, who we affectionately called Momma, was pure joy. I was my grandparent's first-born granddaughter and the only girl for seven years before another girl child would be born. Needless to say, I was spoiled and loved beyond by both my grandparents and family. At the tender age of nine, my mother had two more children my brother, who was six and now new addition, and my baby sister, not even one-year-old yet. After my baby sister was born, we soon moved into an apartment with our dad. I was a big sister and proud of it. I would find out that being a big sister and the eldest child would come with responsibility beyond what a child my age would normally have at nine-year-old. My mom had to work and took an evening job which meant I suddenly became a babysitter and support when mom was at work. I helped my dad with my baby sister in the night, feedings and changing diapers and whatever was needed.

I was a proud big sister and taking care of my siblings gave me great joy; however, it was very taxing on my body as a young girl and I would get little sleep many nights, staying awake with my baby sister, who was an infant needing round the clock care. My parents did not make me watch her; I wanted to do it. In my mind, she was my baby girl, and I treated her like my own precious responsibility. I remember the day she was born; I couldn't wait for her to come home from the hospital. It seemed like forever because she was born premature which was before her due date, and my mom came home first because my sister needed to stay in the hospital for additional care; she was born at 3 pounds 12 ounces. It was a couple of months before she was cleared strong enough to come home. When my mom finally brought my sister home, I was instantly overwhelmed with joy, my baby girl was home, and there was nothing I wouldn't do for her. So helping my dad care for her as my mom worked nights was exciting. My mom would later teach me how to cook, and I was responsible for ensuring that my younger brother and I reached school with the Septa bus. That was a little scary for me, but I was encouraged I could do this, and so I did.

Growing up as a child, one of my biggest obstacles was simply believing and understanding who I was, being comfortable and loving me in my own skin. From a very early age, I noticed that I was unique. And apparently, the other kids knew it too. I got teased a lot, starting with my name. I cried when *Nephetina* was spoken or mispronounced. Every time my name had to be called aloud, I cringed. And so, in the beginning, I hated my name. To add insult to injury, I was told I spoke "too proper"; as an African-American young lady growing up, I got teased for being articulate. And if things weren't already difficult enough, I dressed uniquely. I was a dance major and creatives, no matter what part of artistry we were in, were considered *unique* people. Three strikes, you're out.

My family, especially my mom, always encouraged me to be myself unapologetically without reservation. To always believe in myself, she reminded me that I was not defined by what others thought of me. My grandfather played a huge role in my life, always picking me up and taking me with him, showing me so much love. Many times he would rescue me from home just so I could breathe. Although he never talked about what I was going through, he made sure I knew he was there for me. He played a tremendous part in my receiving salvation at the tender age of twelve. Always reminding me, "Baby, with Christ all things are possible." Granddad, affectionately known as Daddy, was one of my heroes growing up. My family was part of and meant everything to me; their affirmation instilled a sense of confidence to withstand the naysayers. Regardless of the bullying and teasing, I did not lose my self-esteem. I learned to love me more, and I realized that I could not fully love myself while simultaneously living in the shadow of the expectations of others. I had to love who I was, be who I was, and grow through the process.

And throughout childhood, I found myself often doing things on my own, not attracted to big groups or crowds. However, in high school, I had friends and a very diverse group of friends at that. I was blessed with the opportunity to attend a college preparatory performing arts middle and high school where I was a dance major. There I found my tribe, space, and place where my peers accepted me for who I was. It was a supreme feeling, and I found myself loving the exposure to students anywhere from Cambodia to Italy, with so many different nationalities, cultures, and ethnicities I hadn't experienced before.

Reflecting back, one of the most beautiful parts of my upbringing was being able to communicate with and effectively relate to people of various ethnicities and cultures. Those skills would go on to serve me well in the area of counseling and coaching globally as an adult. However, as a teen, I could empathize all too well with those who struggled with the effects of trauma and dysfunction. After all, life wasn't always easy for me, either, even in those impressionable years. Yes, I was cared for, and I had a nice upbringing, a family that loved me; all my needs were met, and I did not want for anything nor did

I ever go lacking. My parents worked hard and instilled that work ethic in all of their children. But no one knew I would go home to an atmosphere of domestic abuse, bringing a whole different dynamic to my life. It wasn't easy. It was extremely challenging.

As a child and teenager, I grappled with the guilt of feeling as if I should have stood up for my mom, if just for the fact that we both were female. But I felt so stuck, steeped in the hurt; I felt deeply for her that I could only internalize it all. That weight of getting up every day and going to school, knowing that when I left home, there was always the possibility that one of my parents would be harmed. All this, while still having to function as a normal teenager, going home to a house that was far from normal. My loneliness was overwhelming at times, feeling like there was no real friend who could possibly understand or even care about what I was going through. It became a very lonely road, carrying the secret of what was really happening within our home underneath a routine and smile, and a heart reeling from the pain my mother endured coupled with what I was experiencing at the hand of a parent that was supposed to care for and protect me. I cannot stand to talk about what I personally was suffering during that time as it is too painful.

I was always a dreamer; as a teenager, I had my own room that faced the airport. I would stand and look out my window, watching the plains fly over my head with the moon shining brightly in the sky. I would daydream of me flying away in those plains to other parts of the world. I innately knew that someday I was going to go to other countries. I envisioned I would travel the world and live far away from home. Part of me wanted just to escape and the other part wanted a new reality from what I was living in currently. I would find myself always praying to God to take me away to a place where I would be accepted for who I was and for all of my differences. I had many dreams of going far away. I often felt I did not belong to my family and that I was adopted and for many years, I would resolve it in my own mind. I was a twin who was separated from her real family. The tricks the enemy plays in our minds are real. Until one day, I would take a good look into the mirror and see my mom, and I knew that thought was only in my mind derived from hurt. I saw me and realized I am my mother's child. I can smile at these thoughts now, but then it was no laughing matter. My heart was broken on so many levels as a child molested with feelings of shame, disappointment, and many nights unable to sleep because I would stare at my room door out of fear. Although I was able to confront my dad many years later, and he apologized repeatedly and sincerely. I was able to forgive him with the help of counselors and my then-boyfriend and current husband. I was able to finally put that part of my life to rest.

I was happy when my mother one day found the strength to leave. But not before I left first. I ran away from home, leaving my last year of high school. Walking away from being an A-student to now being a high school dropout was devastating. My goal was to finish high school, go away to college, to never deal with that life again. But things didn't quite happen the way I planned. I needed to secure a healthy space for me to live and be, with the wisdom even as a youth, to preserve and prioritize my own sanity and well-being. I solemnly promised myself in those low moments of confusion and transition that I would NEVER give up on me. After securing my living situation, I wound up returning to school the next year and finishing. I kept that promise to myself.

Being a teen who worked to support herself while going to school wasn't easy either. However, I persevered and was rewarded with opportunities for doing so. I had already started working at the early age of 14 with the prestigious Mayoral Summer Youth Program. After that, there weren't many jobs that I didn't get on a first interview. That gift of articulation that I was once teased for would actually take me far! From there, my first job was an assistant secretary position in the Counseling and Psychology Department of the elite University of Pennsylvania's Wharton School of Business. And years later, full circle, I am now Dr. Nephetina Serrano, certified Marriage Counselor, Certified Counselor (NBCA) Mentor, Relationship Expert, and Certified Life Coach. All because I dared to DREAM and keep a promise to myself. To never give up on my dreams. I decided to use those lessons learned early on to stand up for myself and be unapologetically me and live out my dreams. I decided to love me and believe in me, regardless of the opinions and expectations of others. I was determined that I was going to make it. One day while in the shower, as I reflected upon Dr. Martin Luther King, Jr. and "I have a dream," it was at that very moment I heard a still voice whisper, "You are the dream walking." So I encourage you never to stop dreaming and never give up on your dreams. I received that word whispered in my ear that day and I passed it on to you, "YOU ARE THE DREAM."

If some way I could go back and speak to my childhood self, I would say lovingly to her, as I say to you: *Girl, rise up and love you more. Do not make apologies or excuses for who you are. You are unique. You are not made to fit in because you are far from average. You were made to stand out, so be free in that. And baby girl, love the skin you are in! God made you beautiful, and He makes no junk! Know God never allow you have a dream that He will not see you to. Never give up on you because you are worth it! Love yourself, really love yourself–because without self-love, it's impossible to love anyone else.* **I AM THE DREAM WAKLKING!**

When I hear my name called these days, I don't cringe or blush in embarrassment. I answer proudly. Unique queen, namely the "beautiful beloved companion." I am not Nefertiti, but I am *Queen Nephetina*, holding my head up in the regal splendor and beauty of who God made me to be, a unique goddess in my own right.

Nephetina's Acknowledgments

First and foremost, I'd like to acknowledge God, who has made this moment possible and is here with me now. He shows me every day that he loves me more than enough. Thank you, Lord, for being the center of my joy and the constant force of all things good in my life. My savior and my deliver in whom I put my trust.

To my Husband and bestie, Minister, Dr. Richard Serrano, you are my biggest supporter, always cheering me on. Thank you for loving all my crazy acts, for all the nights you go to bed without me, praying me through when things get overwhelming. Thank you, my forever love, you lead me in ways you'll never know and I am tremendously blessed to have you in my life. To our daughter, Brande, who has a smile that lights up a room. There is no stop in my love for you. From the day I set eyes on you, that sweet little girl, well, it was an instant bond we shared. I am happy God chose me to be your bonus mom and you are my forever Puddin. Praying God always watches over you and life always be kind to you.

Thank you to every woman who has influenced me along my life's journey. Starting with my Grandmother Emma (Mama) deceased, YOU loved me so much and I am so glad I was able to experience your love and your cooking hence why I love cooking today. To my amazing 4x Degree earner, Mommy Emma Jean Brant M.A.C.C., you taught me never to stop learning and it's never too late to begin again, Aunt Louise (aka Aunt Loudie) for caring for me as your own daughter, you showed me how to be strong, take care of family and never give up, Auntie Quin who was my bestie growing up and always looking out for me, braiding my hair, making my clothes even now and still rescuing me when I need it. Mom Pat (deceased), what can I say? You were love and you gave love; there was never a stepchild in your vocabulary, just daughter. You ladies showed it really does take a village to raise a family. I am everything I am because you all poured into me a little of you.

To my sisters' January, Tanya, and Rosie, you three are part of my why, and I love each of you. My Brothers' Pastor Roosevelt Brant III, Hakim, and Tyre (Deceased) love you guys more than you know, and Ty, I miss you beyond words. My Nieces Tiffany and Alexiis, two beauties who take after their auntie LOL, never give up on your dreams, always have a plan and never stop moving forward. BE THE ONE and always Lead yourself first. My little bundle of joy, the latest edition Ameii Love … you have brought Tio and I so much love, thank you, God. Love your Teti.

Note: A pause for me. I am so proud of myself after the sudden loss of my Dad, the one who raised me, and a war with diabetes that I am determined to win; God has helped me through this project though it has not been an easy assignment to carry out. However, when you are pregnant with purpose and destiny, it is never going to be easy. I encourage you never to abort your purpose; go through the process and let GOD lead you. Never give up on your dreams. I am a witness; God will not let you fail; he will send you people that will hold up your arms, WOG; Momma Emma Jean Brant, Terry Moragne-Macon, Lorraine Martin, Dr. Bernadette Camp, Kim Jacobs, Pastor Uchenna Lewis, Dr. Telishia Berry, Di Cater, Alicia Couri, Andrea Carter, and many others praying for me to succeed people that will pray when you are not looking. For every DREAMER, Never give up on your dream. God is your refuge and very present help in time of need. Remember, You Are the Dream Walking. God promises us the Victory!

To my spiritual family, MT Airy C.O.G.I.C., to my leaders, Bishop J. Louis Felton and Lady Dr. Pricilla Felton, I have learned a lot watching you, and I am a better Servant Leader doing Kingdom work. To my Overseer Bishop Ernest C. Morris Sr., and father in the Gospel for over 33 yrs., and Mother Winifred Morris, what can I say? You are true leaders who lead well and have built a legacy. You have taught me so much over the past 33 years, and I am forever grateful for God putting you both in my life. My husband and I love you both for the Leaders you are and the example you have been; words cannot fully disclose what I feel inside for you and your family, who have been family to us for all these years and continue to show up.

To the amazing visionary of this book anthology, my sister in the Gospel and friend Dr. Kishma George, thank you for showing the world it is not how you start but how you finish. You are making an impact on the earth and around the world that will be felt, talked about, duplicated and celebrated long after we're gone. CONGRATULATIONS! YOU ARE THE DREAM.

Sincerely,

Dr. Nephetina L. Serrano

Serrano Legacy Publishing, LLC

SPECIAL THANKS TO THE FOLLOWING:

YOMI GARNETT, MD ROYAL BIOGRAPHICAL INSTITUTE - CONTRIBUTING EDITOR, BIO PHOTO BY JACKIE HICKS FOND MEMORIES PHOTOGRAPHY, MAKE-UP LETITIA THORNHILL, HAIR MICHELLE SCOFIELD.

Ambassador Dr. Nephetina L. Serrano

Relationship Expert, The Marriage CEO ®

United Nations Global Ambassador for Peace, Relationship Expert, Counselor, International Transformational Speaker, Publisher, Award Winning & Best Selling Author, Evangelist, Certified Life Coach, Mentor, TV Host, Humanitarian.

Dr. Nephetina, United Nations Ambassador for Peace, Woman of Achievement U.S. National Ambassador Queen 2022, and African Women Health Project International Director for the Philadelphia Tristate Global Chapter (PTGC). She is the Chief Publisher of Serrano Legacy Publishing Co. She ensures authors are empowered by publishing compelling stories, establishing a lasting literary legacy in a spirit of integrity, excellence, and love. Dr. Serrano is an International Transformational Speaker, determined, committed influencer, and thought leader who is changing the game and making a difference in the lives of women, girls, and couples globally.

Dr. Serrano has been married to Ambassador Dr. Richard Serrano for over 33 years with one bonus daughter Brande Serrano. They co-founded Covenant Marriages, Inc., Covenant Marriages Institute, and Covenant Rescue 911 501©3 nonprofit 24-hour hotline for couples and families in crisis. They have an outside-the-four-walls ministry, helping couples in transitional phases within their marriage while providing a learning platform for singles preparing to embark on their marital journey. Together with their nonprofit organization, Covenant Rescue 911 to build a 72-hour overnight care oasis facility, the Serranoes' will co-host their new upcoming Television Show, "The Serrano Show," airing on Facebook Live every Thursday at 8 PM EST.

Dr. Nephetina Serrano is an award-winning multiple bestselling author who co-authored and published the book, The Marriage Corporation, highlighting the organizational needs of a covenant marriage. She then launched Marriage CEO Magazine for the Entrepreneur Who Leads, Building Legacy, a publication tailored to meet the relationship needs of couples and individuals, especially those in leadership positions in the community, marketplace, and ministry.

Dr. Serrano has a Doctorate of Philosophy in Business Administration, an Honorary Doctorate in Humanitarian, a Certified Business & Entrepreneurship Coach, a Certified Counselor, and a member of The National Biblical Counseling Association NBCA. Certified Marriage and Relationship Life Coach, Licensed & Ordained Evangelist, and Mentor. She has mentored young women and girls within and outside her community. Dr. Serrano is the Director of African Women Health Project International, AWPHI, Philadelphia Tristate Global Chapter, PTGC, and likewise held positions of Board member and advisor mentor of KISH Home Inc., Big Brothers and Big Sisters, President of Young Women Christian Counsel, and more.

Dr. Serrano has received countless awards and certificates, honoring and acknowledging her Humanitarian contributions nationally and globally; the recipient of the prestigious President's Legacy LIFETIME Achievement Award signed by the 44th President, Barack Obama and the Lifetime Achievement Award 2022 and 2021, signed by President Joe Biden. Courageous Magazine, Top 10 to Watch in 2023. Power UP Summit Entrepreneur of the YEAR 2022, G9 Global Icon Award Dubai 2022, Success Magazine named her one of the 100 Best Life Coaches of 2021, and The City Council for the City of Philadelphia honored her with a CITATION recognizing her contribution to women. The Echoes of Africa, Mayor Commission on African and Caribbean Immigrant Affairs, The SIMA Global Award, Women of Wealth Award, Publishers Golden Eagle Award, Women of Achievement U.S. National Ambassador Crown and Platform Award, ACHI Magazine Woman of Inspiration Award 2019. The State of California SENATE recognition in honor of GSFE Senator Richard D. Roth 31st District California Legislature Assembly Game Changer Award, Assembly Member 61st District Jose Medina 2021 County of Riverside Influencer Award, County of Los Angeles California Commendation Dedicated Service to Community Award Supervisor, First District Hilda L. Solis, Catalyst for Change Girls with Pearls Award and many more.

Dr. Serrano's other best-selling books include RISE UP Women Who Lead Building Legacy, Make It Happen, No Matter What You Can Make It, This Is How I Fight My Battles, The Price of Greatness and Trailblazers Who Lead II Unsung Heroes, other books include, When Doves Cry-Stories That Heal, Stilettos Stand Diaries Exposed,

The Birthing Place Five-Fold Ministry, Wives on Fire, Ain't No PLAN "B" and, Love Your Haters.

DR. NEPHETINA L. SERRANO

C/o Covenant Rescue 911

www.marriageCEOs360.com

DrSerranoministries@gmail.com

116 BALA AVE, SUITE 1B, BALA CYNWYD, PA 19004

The Vision: To encourage, uplift, and inspire you to rise, move forward into your destiny and God-ordained purpose, model the way for the next generation of young women, and teach them no matter how hard you fall, you must not stay there. Dr. Serrano supports couples to achieve balance and stability in life and business through biblical principles and to build more effective communication in their marriage and relationship. Dr. Serrano's vision, build a 72-hour overnight care oasis for a couple or family in crisis, a place where couples can receive the necessary urgent care, heal, be restored, find peace, and be provided with the tools to rebuild and continue the journey toward oneness and forever. Her motto is: "Save a marriage, Save a community."

It Will Happen For You

Shamika Minisee

There is a MIGHTY collision coming!

COLLIDE- verb col·lide | \ kə-ˈlīd \

Definition of collide 1 : to come together with solid or direct impact

Prepare yourself because some of you are about to witness the actual manifestation of your prayers, efforts, and desires! Your sacrifices & prayers WEREN'T FOR NOTHING!

I'm telling you, the thing you've been waiting for has also been waiting on you. What you have been searching for and praying for has also been searching and praying for you!

The Lord will make it happen – Isaiah 60:22

There is no need to cry or be depressed over what does not appear to be occurring right now. Please do not be concerned with what is going on in the lives of others. Look inside! Your blessing is with you, within you, and will be revealed in due time. Do not be afraid! What is going to happen to you will have you REJOICING that it did not happen the way you wanted or with WHO you thought it would happen with, but according to God's plan and in God's time! You can be certain that it will be deliberate and solid!

There's a video that I absolutely love, and it's a video of a man talking to someone through the window. Now, if you look with judgmental eyes, you would believe that this man is off of his rocker based on his appearance. However, what he says resonates with me and all that I do. He tells the person in the car that they need to be thinking big and he repeats it a few more times, getting louder and louder and then walking off. At this point, you may be wondering how this applies to me? Why did he say this to the person in the car and simply walk off after? Because, he meant it, said it enough times, and was done with what he had to say. No need to overcook the grits, as my friend Annie would say.

What matters is if you have a dream and believe with all of your heart and work towards realizing that dream, you have to also believe that it will happen for you! Life doesn't happen to you; it happens for you. Your trials and your blessings are the same thing.

Jim Carrey says, "When I say life doesn't happen to you, it happens for you, I really don't know if that's true. I'm just making a conscious choice to perceive challenges as something beneficial so that I can deal with them in the most productive way."

Sometimes you won't have the words to speak to who you're called to because of who you are becoming.

You are still developing the language, mindset, attitude, lifestyle, and solution. Once you become, you will know what to say and who to say it to. They will hear, feel, and respond to your frequency accordingly. You are being reset, so right now, you may feel out of place. Anything being shaken up, NEVER lands the same way! Truthfully speaking, you've maxed out the level you're on. Take the L's (lessons) and rebuild. Take it easy, beloved; the life you've been praying for is already in motion.

As a professional, smart woman of faith, you've got desires in your heart and goals to pursue. In order to succeed and attain our goals in today's world, we must keep ourselves motivated. We must believe in the strength of our dreams and God's promises every day. That is what will keep us going when things become difficult.

Choosing to follow our dreams is not an easy journey. Sure, we have good days, even great days. But truth be told, we have tough days, too. So when the going gets tough, what does God want us to do?

> *"Ask of me, and I will make the nations your heritage,*
> *and the ends of the earth your possession."*
> *Psalm 2:8*

Women of Faith to Dream BIG Remember:

1 – You have to know it's possible.

Surround yourself with others who are pursuing their goals. Collaborate with those who are already pursuing your goals. When you see their outcomes, you'll think, "If they can do it, I can too!" Success is contagious. Take inspiration from their tales as you listen to them. Examine the hints left by their success. But be careful not to contrast their beginning with your midway. Everyone has a beginning. Since you've seen others accomplish their goals, you can start exactly where you are and are certain that you can too. Surround yourself with others who are already doing what you want to do. Seeing their results will cause you to say, "If they can do it, I can too!" Success breeds success. Listen to their stories and let them inspire you. Pick up the clues their success leaves behind. But remember not to compare their middle to your beginning. Everyone starts somewhere. You can start right where you are, knowing that it's possible because you've seen others do what you want to do.

2 – Think Bigger.

How big of a dreamer are you? You must allow your thoughts to visualize a future worth living if you want to realize your dreams. Your imagination, which is an act of will, is where it all begins. Do you have the desire to see your dreams come true?

When you mix your imagination with your faith and dedication, nothing can stop you. The courage that arises inside of you as a result of imagination makes you an unstoppable force.

> *Ephesians 3:20 reads, "Now to Him who is able to do exceedingly abundantly above all that we ask or think…"*

Because of this, we might infer that God desires for us to have expansive minds and that we should do the same.

The Amplified version of this passage is my FAVORITE:

> *"Now to Him Who, by (in consequence of) the [action of His] power that is at work within us, is able to do super abundantly, far over and above all that we [dare] ask*

> *or think [infinitely beyond our highest prayers, desires, thoughts, hopes, or dreams]..."*

Dreaming big is extremely valuable in life since it enables an individual to push themselves past the limit. For example, Oprah Winfrey grew up poor and was abused as a young girl. Although she grew up in a harsh environment, she did not allow that to stop her from pursuing her passion. Needless to say, her efforts were not fruitless, as she became one of the most well-known faces in history. If Lady O had no dream nor worked towards becoming the woman she is today, it is safe to say that she would hold no relevance in today's society. This entertains the thought that challenging oneself to strive for what they think is worth the risk is an important aspect of life.

> *"And let us not grow weary of doing good, for in due season we will reap if we do not give up." (Galatians 6:9, ESV).*

Even while I'm asleep, I'm passionate about women becoming our families' primary dreamers and providers. Future prospects for my children depend on my resolve. Women have a lot of responsibilities, but we also have a lot of gifts. Our vision matters when it comes to how we move toward our calling, how we envision our future, and how we make plans for financial security. Put me in the company of women who have faith and are prepared to work hard. This advancement is merited by our family.

Sometimes it feels like the struggles we face will never end. We seem to be engaged in a futile struggle. Even attempting to recover from the pandemic's consequences has been difficult. What if these uncertain times hide something more valuable? What if God is using those words that someone said to stop you from being what you should be in order to move you forward further than you have ever been? My friend, the trying time you've been through will provide you access to more than you could have ever dreamed. It elevates your degree of accomplishment, which is so profoundly transformative that you will encourage countless people to have even greater dreams.

What goes on behind the scenes is not comparable to what we see on the outside. Even when you are battling, someone can see your bravery. While people praise your devotion to God, you are worn out. It is not how your narrative ends, beloved, since the Lord has planned something better and will elevate the blessings on your labors to much higher levels. Unknown people's lives that you are affecting will never be the same. Despite exceeding your expectations, you haven't yet witnessed anything. Prepare yourself for God to push you over your limitations.

God is able to do exceedingly and abundantly above ALL you can ever ask or think.

DREAM BIGGER!

IMAGINE BIGGER!

CLAIM BIGGER!

BELIEVE BIGGER

If your dreams don't scare you, they're not big enough. There are no limits to what God can do, so don't limit yourself either. You're not here to just pay bills and die! There is PURPOSE over your life. Please, stop agonizing over the unknown. Stop wondering if it will happen or work out. We can't predict the future but FOR SURE, His promises remain the same! God is faithful and you are His child. Keep moving forward and walking in your purpose! Grace and mercy shall follow you ALL the days of your life! That "thing" is coming!

WHAT ARE YOU TRUSTING GOD FOR?

Shamika's Acknowledgements

With my deepest gratitude, I'd like to acknowledge **my husband**, who I've seen grow weary but never faint, who's shown me so much strength and grace in our faith walk and marriage, who's helped me realize so many dreams, and who's prayed for me when I couldn't pray. Also, **my children**, who have unshakable faith and work for what they believe in. **My darling mother** who simply let me be. Her giving me the wings to fly equipped me to become all that I am. I'm forever grateful that she never let me change my heart and believed in my dreams. And to **my angel** who loved me on Earth and in heaven. I'm so thankful that our paths crossed. He'd lovingly cheer me on and often tell me, "We all we got." **My darling brother**, I know you see me. I would also like to thank and acknowledge **Pastor Kishma George** for seeing me, extending an olive branch and believing in me. And last and certainly not least, **God,** I thank you; God, I yield to you, and I love you. Thank you for sitting me down in this season and handing me every brick I needed to see myself. Because of you, I acknowledge and encourage every dreamer who picks this devotional up never to stop dreaming. Those dreams are your reality.

Shamika M. Minisee

Shamika Minisee is CEO and co-founder of Presidential Concrete LLC and The Minisee Group and is on a mission to help women build and grow profitable careers and companies. Trained as a contracting professional, she has a unique 17-year background in strategic planning, communications, leadership, acquisition management on multi-billion development projects, research, professional writing, and business development, providing her clients with unique advantages.

As an empowerment expert dedicated to helping others fully embrace their power and honor their potential, Shamika brings a dynamic and motivational message delivered with humor, passion and inspiration. She has the makings of a major business entity with the persona, wit, and credentials to back it up. As a self-made entrepreneur, she has a knack for focusing on incorporating lessons learned supporting the armed forces and process improvement in construction, engineering services and the mortgage industry while seeking employment and growing businesses.

With motivation, high-energy and poise, Shamika's WHY is to inspire, uplift and push career-driven individuals and to help business CEOs create better blueprints, business, experiences and lives. Working on a wide range of assignments from Human Resources Research to Counter-Narcotics Anti-Terrorism, Major Items/Engineering Services, Integrated Air and Missile Defense, Health & Wellness, Construction & AMP, Process Engineering, to name a few. She's able to deliver her unique range of innovative solutions across industries and appeal to mass audiences. A native of St. Louis, Missouri, Shamika relocated to Huntsville, Alabama, on her quest for higher education and now resides there with her husband Jason and their three children, Jayden, Payton and Jason Jr. She holds a Bachelor's degree in Business Administration and Management Information Systems from Alabama A&M University as well as a Master's in Management & AMP; Acquisition/Contract Management from Florida Institute of Technology. Memberships include Delta Sigma Theta Sorority Incorporated, Huntsville Free Dental Clinic Advisory Board, and Sickle Cell Leadership Consortium National Board. In her spare time, she helps people with personal development services, which include resume writing, business marketing and planning, and job search and placement opportunities.

Let's stay in touch: linktr.ee/shamikaminisee

Seven Keys to Dream Management & Stewardship

Dr. Nicckay Natson

And they said one to another, Behold, this dreamer cometh." Genesis 37:19-21

I want to give you seven keys to awaken the dreamer in you.

These are Seven Keys that will help propel you into your destiny and purpose for your dreams and help you stay focused on stewarding the dream that God gave you.

 # 1 Spend time with Him before you have to deal with them. (In ministry or in business) get delivered from people. You will begin to allow people to dictate your value and worth. You have to know who you are and your own value and worth. You were sent to help them, not for them to hinder you. Spend time with him so he can help you deal with them.

Genesis 50:21 (AMP)

Just as God had sent Joseph ahead to Egypt so he could be in position to comfort and give hope and strength to his starving family in Canaan, God knows the future and has our backs. We can't always see it but if we believe it … we will see it.

If we can turn our attention away from the outside pressures and focus our attention and trust in the One who made heaven and earth, our perspective will change and we won't be robbed of our peace.

God says, 'do not be afraid; I will provide for and support you. . .be comforted by imparting cheer, hope and strength' to others. Psalm 94:19

So don't allow doubts to fill your mind.

2 Determine To Do Something About Your Dreams Every Day.

Proverbs 16:3 (AMP)
"Roll your works upon the Lord [commit and trust them wholly to Him; He will cause your thoughts to become agreeable to His will, and] so shall your plans be established and succeed."

When our thoughts line up with the Word of God. . .He will cause our plans to be successful.

Psalm 20:4 (NLT):
"May he grant your heart's desires and make all your plans succeed."

A dream without a plan is just wishful thinking.

It's important to create visual and audible reminders about the steps you need to take on a daily basis to turn your dreams into reality.

List the action steps and reminders in your electronic data retrieval system (smartphone or tablet). Write these steps in your planner . . . post them on your refrigerator. . even on the mirror you use to get ready for work each day.

If you hear a sermon. . .read a book. . .listen to a CD that motivates you toward your goal. . .keep it in front of you. We must always visualize where we want to go and what we intend to do along the way.

 # 3 Increase the Possibility of Success with These Daily Questions.

Every morning ask God to open your eyes and reveal the answer to these questions:

What can I do today to learn something I didn't know yesterday?

What can I do today to increase my skill set?

What can I do today to renew my determination?

What can I do today to make a divine connection?

What can I do today to keep my dream of success in front of me?

What can I do today to improve on what I've been doing?

And most importantly, what can I do today to draw closer to You, Lord, and deeper into the revelation of Your Word?

If you were wondering how you can possibly manifest the answers. . .may I suggest a careful reading of Proverbs 3:5-6 in The Living Bible which says:

"If you want favor with both God and man, and a reputation for good judgment and common sense, then trust the Lord completely; don't ever trust yourself. In everything you do, put God first, and he will direct you and crown your efforts with success."

Continue to trust God to provide the answers. What 'seems' impossible to you … is never impossible to Him.

4 Become an Expert in Your Field.

If you read one hour a day about something you know nothing about…within one year, you will be an expert in your city. Within two years…you will be an expert in your state. And within five years, you will be an international expert.

…be determined to learn and do what you've never known or done.

After all … these statistics concern a subject you 'know nothing about.' If your desire is to be outstanding in your field of endeavor… you have a huge head start already.

With a little more effort, you will achieve your goal with amazing speed. The more intense your commitment to gaining new wisdom…the more God will honor your hard work and effort.

1 Corinthians 3:10 (AMP):
"According to the grace (the special endowment for my task) of God bestowed on me, like a skillful architect and master builder I laid [the] foundation, and now another

> *[man] is building upon it. But let each [man] be careful how he builds upon it."*

As you become an expert in your field of interest and/or in the Word of God . . . remember your growth is built line upon line.

> *Isaiah 28:10 says:*
> *"For precept must be upon precept, precept upon precept; line upon line, line upon line; here a little, and there a little."*

To make your dream a reality. . .you must be a learner. . .if you ever want to be a bigger earner. Concentrate on the learning … and the earning will come on its own.

#5 Be Creative in Overcoming Roadblocks, Obstacles and Detours.

Once you determine to pursue your dreams with a purpose, passion and plan, you will be met with roadblocks, obstacles and detours. Learn to see these impediments to your success as stages of your success.

> *Psalm 84:6-7 in the Amplified Bible says:*
> *"Passing through the Valley of Weeping (Baca), they make it a place of springs; the early rain also fills [the pools] with blessings. They go from strength to strength [increasing in victorious power]; each of them appears before God in Zion."*

Understand the revelation.

The Valley of Baca, otherwise known as the Valley of Tears, is full of difficulties and trials.

I know we would prefer not having to go through the valley, but I can assure you that making this trip will leave you stronger and poised even more for success.

We must recognize the absolute necessity of having God direct our paths in overcoming all the roadblocks of life.

Accept temporary mistakes, detours and disappointments as just that, temporary. Learn from every mistake and move forward, no looking back or blaming anyone.

How do you overcome obstacles?

Psalm 34:19 (NCV):
"People who do what is right may have many problems, but the Lord will solve them all."
Tell God what you're facing. . .ask Him how to handle it.

Psalm 142:2 in the New Century Version says:
"I pour out my problems to him; I tell him my troubles."
Exodus 18:19 (NIV):
"Listen to me. I'll give you some advice, and may God be with you. You must speak to God for the people. Take their problems to him."

When you face roadblocks, obstacles and detours, turn to the One who will cause you to never lose your way as you move toward your new reality.

 # 6 Stop Procrastination, Leave Procrastination at Your Front Door.

Knowing and doing. . .keeping procrastination out of your life. . . is essential to turning your dreams into a new reality.

Ecclesiastes 3:11 in the Message Bible says:
"There's an opportune time to do things, a right time for everything on the earth."
Someone said once:
"Never put off until tomorrow . . *what you can do today."*

Procrastination is defined in Webster's New World Dictionary as:

"To put off doing something until a future time; to postpone or defer taking action."

Are you a procrastinator? Here are ten questions to help you determine if you're a procrastinator:

1. Do you wait until the last minute to undertake an important task, duty or assignment?

2. Do you buy birthday and anniversary cards and presents on the day of the celebration?

3. Do you postpone and reschedule doctor and dentist appointments?

4. Do you make up excuses why certain small assignments haven't been completed?

5. Do you wait until Christmas week to buy presents for your loved ones?

6. Do you always get an extension for filing your income tax return?

7. Do you constantly postpone your plans to clean out the attic, garage or your desk?

8. Do you delay calling creditors about disputes on your monthly statements?

9. Do you forget until the deadline has expired before sending in the rebate slip from a purchase you've made?

10. Do you avoid scheduling difficult conversations with family members, your supervisor or fellow employees?

If you answered "yes" to three or more of the above questions. . .then you are, in fact, a procrastinator or have procrastinator tendencies. If you are one. . . STOP IT NOW!

You will never achieve the success God intended for you to achieve if you procrastinate.

You have a choice. . .you can either follow your dreams and do something about it.

"I'm going to stop putting things off ... until tomorrow."

Or you can follow the Word of God. Proverbs 6:4 in the New Living Translation says:

> *"Don't put it off; do it now! Don't rest until you do."*
> Whatever you need to do ... do it without delay.

 # 7 Be Ready To Help Others. What God placed in you is not for you but for someone else.

The best way to make your dreams come true is to help someone else make their dreams come true.

Ephesians 6:8 says:
"Knowing that whatsoever good thing any man doeth, the same shall he receive of the Lord, whether he be bond or free."

Bottom line. . .**if you want happiness in your life. . .then sow happiness into the lives of others**.

Sadly, there are people who want happiness. . .but have never sown the first seed of happiness.

If you want your dreams to come true. . .ask God to use you to help others make their dreams come true.

God will do for you what you've done for them.

The New International Version of Ephesians 6:8 says:

"The Lord will reward everyone for whatever good he does. . ."

If you want to be rewarded. . .paid and blessed. . .then make it your business. . .your mission. . .your passion to help other people achieve their dreams.

When you become a Dream Maker for someone else. . .God will do the same for you.

Start today living out your dreams……

Isaiah 43:19 in the Message Bible says:
"Be alert, be present. I'm about to do something brand-new. It's bursting out! Don't you see it? There it is! I'm making a road through the desert, rivers in the badlands."

Regardless of what you perceive to be your limitations. . .God is ready for you to experience a new beginning at this very moment.

Micah 4:7 (NLV):
"I will make a new beginning with those who cannot walk. I will make a strong nation of those who have been driven away. And the Lord will rule over them in Mount Zion from that day and forever."

It's time to stop talking and start doing. It's even time to stop praying and get moving.

Exodus 14:15 (TLB):
"Then the Lord said to Moses, 'Quit praying and get the people moving! Forward, march!'"

Today. Right now. . .this very moment is the best time. . .the right time for you to decide enough is enough.

This is your defining moment when you will decide that you're not going to live the way you've been living anymore.

In defining moments like this. . .you make a decision to change things.

You realize your financial environment will not change until you change. . .and you will not change. . .until you change the way you think.

Romans 12:2 (NLT)
"Let God transform you into a new person by changing the way you think."

It's moments like this when you realize the power available to you through scriptures like Ephesians 3:20 in the Amplified Bible, which says:

"Now to Him Who, by (in consequence of) the [action of His] power that is at work within us, is able to [carry out His purpose and] do superabundantly, far over and above all that we [dare] ask or think [infinitely beyond our highest prayers, desires, thoughts, hopes, or dreams]."

You need to realize this is your time. . .this is your day. . .now is your time.

Yes, make no mistake about it. . .**Now is the time. . .don't wait. . .don't procrastinate. . .activate your dreams. And don't allow the devil to steal, kill or rob you of your dreams.**

Ecclesiastes 11:1 (TLB):
"If you wait for perfect conditions, you'll never get anything done."

One more thing. . .you've got to stop looking at the past.

If you dwell on past hurts, failures, broken relationships and financial mistakes, then you're doomed to repeat them.

Isaiah 43:18 in the Message Bible says:
"Forget about what's happened; don't keep going over old history."

Here's a fact...**God can't do a new thing in your life as long as your living in the past.** Don't commiserate about what happened...instead plan on how to turn your dreams into a new reality.

Dr. Nicckay's Acknowledgements

Thank you to my mentor **Dr. Kishma George** for never giving up so many years ago and giving God a real yes. Thank you for believing in me and seeing greatness in me and always encouraging and pushing me to go forward. Thank you to my husband of 26 years, **Apostle Alton T. Natson**, for being my best friend, my rider and my purpose partner who has always believed in me and encouraged me every day to be the unique person that God designed me to be. My number one supporter, thank you from the top, bottom and center of my heart. **My children** and **grandchildren,** who keep the fire burning within and remind me daily about the legacy and trans-generational blessings and the history being rewritten every day as I give God my authentic yes. **My spiritual children** for their love, honor and unselfishly giving their support. **The Forerunners Center** and **KGAN Family**, you all are phenomenal; thank you for your push and believing in me.

My Personal Intercessors who pray for me daily, even covering me in this project and praying for my family, businesses and ministries, thank you so much; I don't take it lightly. My mentor **Prophetess Kendria Moore** for seeing something in me that many people don't see. She reminds me that the scars I carry qualifies me for the nations that I am not local but global, and the open doors and favor that's upon my life is well deserved. I also want to acknowledge my spiritual mother, **Apostle Sarafina Marvin,** who always speaks life over me and encourages me to keep pushing and telling me that greatness is on the inside of me. Reminding me that I could do whatever I put my mind to even when I felt like giving up.

To **Apostle Ron Toliver,** thank you for the pour and for reminding me that I am a part of a new breed, a generation for generations that will pierce darkness and overthrow hell's plans through the ministry and gifts that God has given me.

Dr. Nicckay Natson

Dr. Nicckay is an Apostle, Teacher and Prophet of God. She is the founder of Alton and Nicckay Natson Global Inc. (ANNGI) and Kingdom Global Alliance Network alongside her husband, Apostle Alton Natson. She is also the Apostle of The Forerunners Center, an apostolic center that she and her husband planted in Petersburg, Virginia. She is also the Apostolic Marriage & Family Director of Alton And Nicckay Natson Global Inc alongside her husband, Apostle Alton Natson, where their pulpit is the world.

Dr. Nicckay has been awarded an iconic leading lady award presented by WWT Women Without Titles (Founder: Prophetess Felicia Johnson) for being a woman that does great things but has been overlooked. She has also been awarded by Shekinah Global Ministries (Founder: Apostle Dr. Doris Riley) an award for her leadership role and mentorship programs. She has also been awarded by Lady Capri Ministries (Founder: Dr. Nikia Eason) for being a woman of vision for her leadership and excellence. She has been featured in God Lock Magazine, on the front cover of UPWORDS Magazine in India, on the cover of K.I.S.H Magazine, and featured in the Love Nest Magazine, and featured in many other magazines alongside celebrities and gospel artists and on the

QUEEN Millionaire Podcast, Blossoms of My Life Radio Show, The Kishma George IWORSHIP 96 Radio Show and Faith Focused Finish Radio Talk Show, Monica Floyd Ministries Broadcast, Bust A Move Radio Talk Show, The Gifted TV Show, and the Get Up Movement Broadcast and many other podcast and radio shows.

Dr. Nicckay is an International Speaker, Radio Talk Show Host, Television Host (Media Personality), spiritual mother, and a mentor of many, and she provides a spiritual covering for her sons and daughters in the faith and those in the five fold ministry. God has graced her to be a watchman/intercessor and a teacher of intercessors. She is an apostolic and prophetic teacher, a voice and a seer, a pioneer, one who blazes the trail for the Body of Christ and in the marketplace without compromise. A loving wife, mother and friend, her husband describes her as his "Heart Beat" and his Proverbs 31 Woman: [11] The heart of her husband doth safely trust in her, so that he shall have no need of spoil. [12] She will do him good and not evil all the days of her life. Dr. Nicckay earned a Bachelor's Degree in Psychology and Organizational Management in 2007 and a Master's in Executive Leadership and Human Services with a concentration in Marriage and Family Counseling in 2012.

In 2016 she earned a Doctor of Clinical Counseling and Psychology. Additionally, Dr. Nicckay is the co-author of Daughters of Triumph, Overdue, Letters to my Legacy, Unshakable Faith, and Urgency Prayers Right Now, the author of The Birthing of A Intercessor, Lifting the Mask, The Pure In Heart: a 31-day devotional, The Love Nest Marriage Devotional for couples after God's own heart. She is a serial entrepreneur, a leading lady, one who knows how to operate and flow in the kingdom and the marketplace with grace. Before she owned her own businesses, she worked for 20-plus years and wore many different hats, from early childhood educator to principal, from director to mentor director, training and teaching leaders and managers how to be effective at leadership and organizational management building systems, creating policies for business consultants and coaching for the government were she coached, advised, consulted and mentored over 40 sites for the government on a regional level, from that to a Behavior Analyst to a lead mental health therapist to a therapist supervisor and clinical director. One day her husband said to her that he wanted her to come off of the job and work on the things that God had birth and placed within her for them.

Dr. Nicckay is also the Founder and President of Natson Enterprise, L.I.F.T (Ladies In Faith Together) International Inc. A global network for women beyond the four walls of the church, a ministry that empowers, equips, and educates, and a platform for women in ministry and in the marketplace, along with various other things with the belief that her pulpit is the world. She is the President/Founder of Rejuvenation Counseling, Coaching Healing Center & Training Institute LLC, Zenith TV Network, Zenith Radio Network, Bridge Builders University, Pneuma Gifts & Accessories, and Natson Publishing & Creatives LLC, The Love Nest, The Love Nest Magazine for married couples, and singles desiring to be married along with her husband, Flourish Women Magazine, The Awakening Prayer Live/Kingdom Snipers Global Network for Intercessors, Watchman, Gatekeepers and Prayer Warriors, Kingdom Talk Broadcast Radio Show (KTB), Flourish Women Unapologetically Becoming A Better Me Podcast, Flourish

Women TV, Flourish Women Coaching Academy and the co-founder of Spirit of Excellence Resume Service, Revive Credit Restoration.

Dr. Nicckay is a Licensed Clinical Christian Psychologist, Licensed Clinical Christian Therapist, Licensed Christian Marriage & Family Therapist, Certified Professional Life Coach, and Certified Professional Mentor, helping families resolve the complexities of life through professional Christian counseling, coaching, mentoring, inner healing & deliverance. Dr. Nicckay is known as a powerhouse that speaks the truth. She is bold in her approach; although she is bold and dynamic, she walks in love toward others. She is called to the rejected, unchurched, wounded, and those that have been dropped and harbor the spirit of an orphan. She loves to encourage others to walk out their God-given purpose and to be authentic and confident in who God has called them to be. Healing and deliverance are the portions of many that have experienced this vessel's ministry. Dr. Nicckay doesn't look for the movement; she is the movement and the shift in the earth that upsets darkness and shakes up hell.

Her mantra is "We Rise by Lifting Others and her goal and objective is to help others grow in their relationship with the Lord, to dominate in the arena of the 7 mountains of influence that God has given to them to teach, instruct, educate and train others how to possesses the Deuteronomy 8:18 life. Each of us should use whatever gift we received to serve others as faithful stewards of God's grace in its various forms." (1 Peter 4:10) She is the proud mother of two jewels in Christ: Tiannah and Jareal, and the proud glam-ma of Joshua, Joell, Ellianna, and Limmie.

Connect with Dr. Nicckay:

Email Address: drnicckaynatson@gmail.com

Website: www.drnicckaynatson.com

www.luvnest.org, www.kgan.org

Facebook: Apostle Dr. Nicckay Natson @drnicckaynatson, @ANNGINC

Twitter: @DrNicckayNatson

Instagram: @DrNicckayNatson, @kingdomglobalalliancenetwork

Made in the USA
Middletown, DE
22 September 2023

38831576R00066